LEADER'S GUIDE

TO

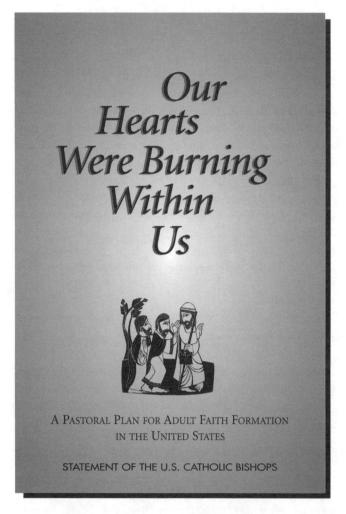

Our Hearts Were Burning Within Us

A PASTORAL PLAN FOR ADULT FAITH FORMATION
IN THE UNITED STATES

STATEMENT OF THE U.S. CATHOLIC BISHOPS

DEPARTMENT OF EDUCATION

UNITED STATES CONFERENCE OF CATHOLIC BISHOPS
WASHINGTON, D.C.

INCLUDES THE PASTORAL PLAN

In 2000 the National Advisory Committee on Adult Religious Education of the Department of Education, United States Catholic Conference, developed this leader's guide for use in conjunction with the U.S. bishops' statement, *Our Hearts Were Burning Within Us: A Pastoral Plan for Adult Faith Formation in the United States*, which was approved on November 17, 1999. The process included consultation with and field testing by dioceses through their Offices of Religious Education. This guide was approved by the chairman of the Committee on Education, Most. Rev. Donald W. Wuerl, and authorized for publication by the undersigned.

Monsignor Dennis M. Schnurr
General Secretary, NCCB/USCC

Acknowledgments: (**project director and general editor**) Jack McBride, Diocese of Madison, Wisconsin; (**senior consultants**) Jim Kemma, Diocese of Jefferson City, Missouri; Deacon John Meyer, Diocese of Phoenix, Arizona; Margaret Ralph, Ph.D., Diocese of Lexington, Kentucky; David Riley, Archdiocese of Cincinnati, Ohio; Sr. Janet Schaeffler, OP, Archdiocese of Detroit, Michigan; Sr. Diane Smith, CSJ, Diocese of Stockton, California; (**pilots**) Edmund Gordon, Diocese of Wilmington, Delaware; Gloria Reinhardt, Diocese of Wilmington, Delaware; Catherine Minkiewicz, Archdiocese of Boston, Massachusetts; Carolyn Saucier, Diocese of Jefferson City, Missouri; David Riley, Archdiocese of Cincinnati, Ohio; Sr. Diane Smith, CSJ, Diocese of Stockton, California; John Meyer, Diocese of Phoenix, Arizona.

First Printing, October 2000
Third Printing, October 2001

ISBN 1-57455-342-9

CONTENTS

PART TWO

Our Hearts Were Burning Within Us:

Discussion group leaders and participants are strongly encouraged to read this plan prior to sessions.

PART ONE

LEADER'S GUIDE TO

Our Hearts Were Burning Within Us

INTRODUCTION

We, as the Catholic bishops of the United States, call the Church in our country to a renewed commitment to adult faith formation, positioning it at the heart of our catechetical vision and practice. We pledge to support adult faith formation without weakening our commitment to our other essential educational ministries. This pastoral plan guides the implementation of this pledge and commitment. (*Our Hearts Were Burning Within Us*, no. 6)

Our Hearts Were Burning Within Us: A Pastoral Plan for Adult Faith Formation in the United States (hereafter OHWB) is a clear call to reinvigorate the effort to foster adult faith formation throughout the United States. Dedicated faith communities of adult believers commit themselves to a lifelong journey of understanding their faith, proclaiming their faith, and living their faith. The effort that nurtures the development of this adult faith community must be intentional, organized, and faithful. To this end, the leader's guide will serve as a tool to

- Encourage adults to study the OHWB plan
- Help adults to consider the implications, for their parishes and dioceses, of the plan's goals and objectives
- Provide an opportunity to begin developing strategies to implement the plan in each parish and throughout every diocese in the United States

Discussion group leaders: You are strongly encouraged to read *Our Hearts Were Burning Within Us: A Pastoral Plan for Adult Faith Formation in the United States*, which begins on page 45 of this guide.

Use this leader's guide in a way that is best suited to you, your parish, and your diocese. You are encouraged to incorporate your own time line, prayers, and questions that reflect your particular circumstances. This leader's guide details a model of three sessions that are each approximately three hours long. Because a three-session option may not be desirable for every diocesan or parish situation, however, outlines of three other options for session lengths are included. You are encouraged to use the option that would be most helpful in your circumstances. The sessions can be facilitated by anyone interested in leading a group through the OHWB plan.

The leader's guide was developed especially for use with such groups as a parish council, education commission, adult formation committee, parish staff, DRE-led group, as well as diocesan offices, committees, and groups.

The hope is that this leader's guide will assist parishes and dioceses in the United States to renew their dedication to adult faith formation, as the OHWB plan inspires all to do:

> Let us strengthen our commitment and intensify our efforts to help the adults in our communities be touched and transformed by the life-giving message of Jesus, to explore its meaning, experience its power, and live in its light as faithful adult disciples today. Let us do our part with creativity and vigor, our hearts aflame with love to empower adults to know and live the message of Jesus. This is the Lord's work. In the power of the Spirit it will not fail but will bear lasting fruit for the life of the world. (OHWB, no. 183)

MULTIPLE OPTIONS FOR SESSIONS

Note to Discussion Group Leaders:

Obviously, one size does not fit everyone. The following options allow you to create a program with the number and length of sessions that best fit your circumstances. The lengths of time listed below are approximate; the session components may be stretched or condensed depending on your group's needs.

> Discussion group leaders: Encourage participants to read the OHWB plan that's included as Part Two of this guide prior to attending your sessions.

To enhance the quality of discussions, you also may want to ask participants to prepare for the sessions by thinking about their parish's adult faith formation efforts over the past few years.

Opening and closing prayers are written for the three-session option that is detailed in this guide. Regardless of the program option you choose for your group, you are encouraged to open and close your sessions with prayer. You may create a prayer that would be appropriate for your gathering or use the opening and closing prayers included in this guide.

I. Three Sessions (3 hours each)

Session One: Focusing on Adult Faith Formation
- Welcome and Opening Prayer (15 minutes)
- Introduction (20 minutes)
- Personal Experience (20 minutes)
- Signs of the Times (30 minutes)
- Break (10 minutes)
- Fostering Mature Faith (30 minutes)
- Goals and Principles (30 minutes)
- Closing Prayer (10 minutes)

Session Two: The What and How of Adult Faith Formation
- Opening Prayer (10 minutes)
- Current Parish Efforts (5 minutes)
- Questions and Concerns About Life and Faith (35 minutes)
- Six Content Areas (20 minutes)
- Break (10 minutes)
- Further Exploration (20 minutes)
- Comparing Notes (10 minutes)
- Approaches to Adult Faith Formation (20 minutes)
- Thinking Differently (20 minutes)
- Closing Prayer (15 minutes)

Session Three: Organizing for Adult Faith Formation
- Opening Prayer (10 minutes)
- The Pivotal Importance of the Parish (30 minutes)
- Key Parish Roles of Leadership and Service:
  - Objective One (15 minutes)
  - Objective Two (20 minutes)
  - Objective Three (20 minutes)
  - Objective Four (20 minutes)
- Identifying the Next Steps (30 minutes)
- Sending-Forth Prayer (10 minutes)

II. Two Sessions (3½–4 hours each)
Session One (4 hours)
- Welcome and Opening Prayer (15 minutes)
- Introduction (20 minutes)
- Personal Experience (20 minutes)
- Signs of the Times (30 minutes)
- Fostering Mature Faith (30 minutes)
- Goals and Principles (30 minutes)
- Current Parish Efforts (5 minutes)
- Questions and Concerns About Life and Faith (35 minutes)
- Six Content Areas (20 minutes)
- Further Exploration (20 minutes)
- Comparing Notes (10 minutes)
- Closing Prayer (5 minutes)

Session Two (3½ hours)
- Opening Prayer (10 minutes)
- Approaches to Adult Faith Formation (20 minutes)
- Thinking Differently (20 minutes)
- The Pivotal Importance of the Parish (30 minutes)
- Break (10 minutes)
- Key Parish Roles of Leadership and Service:
  - Objective One (15 minutes)
  - Objective Two (20 minutes)
  - Objective Three (20 minutes)
  - Objective Four (20 minutes)
- Identifying the Next Steps (30 minutes)
- Sending-Forth Prayer (15 minutes)

III. Four Sessions (1½–2½ hours each)

Session One (2½ hours)
- Welcome and Opening Prayer (15 minutes)
- Introduction (20 minutes)
- Personal Experience (20 minutes)
- Signs of the Times (30 minutes)
- Fostering Mature Faith (30 minutes)
- Closing Prayer (5 minutes)

Session Two (1½ hours)
- Opening Prayer (10 minutes)
- Goals and Principles (30 minutes)
- Current Parish Efforts (5 minutes)
- Questions and Concerns (35 minutes)
- Closing Prayer (10 minutes)

Session Three (2 hours)
- Opening Prayer (10 minutes)
- Six Content Areas (20 minutes)
- Further Exploration (20 minutes)
- Comparing Notes (10 minutes)
- Break (10 minutes)
- Approaches to Adult Faith Formation (20 minutes)
- Thinking Differently (20 minutes)
- Closing Prayer (10 minutes)

Session Four (2½ hours)
- Opening Prayer (5 minutes)
- The Pivotal Importance of the Parish (30 minutes)
- Key Parish Roles of Leadership and Service:
    - Objective One (15 minutes)
    - Objective Two (20 minutes)
    - Objective Three (20 minutes)
    - Objective Four (20 minutes)
- Identifying the Next Steps (30 minutes)
- Sending-Forth Prayer (10 minutes)

IV. Five Sessions (1½–1¾ hours)

Session One (1½ hours)
- Welcome and Opening Prayer (15 minutes)
- Introduction (20 minutes)
- Personal Experience (20 minutes)
- Signs of the Times (30 minutes)
- Closing Prayer (5 minutes)

Session Two (1½ hours)
- Opening Prayer (10 minutes)
- Fostering Mature Faith (30 minutes)
- Goals and Principles (30 minutes)
- Current Parish Efforts (5 minutes)
- Closing Prayer (15 minutes)

Session Three (1¾ hours)
- Opening Prayer (5 minutes)
- Questions and Concerns (20 minutes)
- Six Content Areas (20 minutes)
- Further Exploration (20 minutes)
- Comparing Notes (10 minutes)
- Approaches to Adult Faith Formation (20 minutes)
- Closing Prayer (10 minutes)

Session Four (1½ hours)
- Opening Prayer (10 minutes)
- Thinking Differently (20 minutes)
- The Pivotal Importance of the Parish (30 minutes)
- Key Parish Roles of Leadership and Service:
  Objective One (15 minutes)
- Closing Prayer (15 minutes)

Session Five (1¾ hours)
- Opening Prayer (5 minutes)
- Key Parish Roles of Leadership and Service:
  Objective Two (20 minutes)
  Objective Three (20 minutes)
  Objective Four (20 minutes)
- Identifying the Next Steps (30 minutes)
- Sending-Forth Prayer (10 minutes)

SESSION ONE
FOCUSING ON ADULT FAITH FORMATION

Objectives

At the conclusion of Session One, the participants will have

- Reviewed and understood the general purpose and goals of *Our Hearts Were Burning Within Us: A Pastoral Plan for Adult Faith Formation in the United States* (hereafter OHWB)
- Understood the meaning of adult faith formation—its goals and principles—as presented in the OHWB plan
- Understood the Church's need to emphasize adult faith formation at this moment in history
- Reflected on their personal experience of and need for adult faith formation
- Named the challenges and opportunities for adult faith formation in their parish
- Listed some of the ways that their parish can address the challenges of faith formation in adulthood
- Understood the qualities of mature faith and the nature of mature Christian discipleship as well as some specific ways that communities can foster it

Welcome (5 minutes)

Take a moment to introduce yourself to others around you before praying together.

Opening Prayer (10 minutes)

The Appearance on the Road to Emmaus

"Were not our hearts burning [within us] while he spoke to us on the way and opened the scriptures to us?" (Lk 24:32)

Leader: We are gathered here in God's name. We know that Christ is in our midst. We give thanks for the many and continuous ways that God walks with us. Sometimes we are like the disciples on the road to Emmaus, not readily or immediately recognizing God's presence.

Reader: A reading from the Gospel of Luke (24:13-32):

Now that very day two of them were going to a village seven miles from Jerusalem called Emmaus, and they were conversing about all the things that had occurred. And it happened that while they were conversing and debating, Jesus himself drew near and walked with them, but their eyes were prevented from recognizing him. He asked them, "What are you discussing as you walk along?" They stopped, looking downcast. One of them, named Cleopas, said to him in reply, "Are you the only visitor to Jerusalem who does not know of the things that have taken place there in these days?" And he replied to them, "What sort of things?" They said to him, "The things that happened to Jesus of Nazarene, who was a prophet mighty in deed and word before God and all the people, how our chief priests and rulers both handed him over to a sentence of death and crucified him. But we were hoping that he would be the one to redeem Israel; and besides all this, it is now the third day since this took place. Some women from our group, however, have astounded us: they were at the tomb early in the morning and did not find his body; they came back and reported that they had indeed seen a vision of angels who announced that he was alive. Then some of those with us went to the tomb and found things just as the women had described, but him they did not see." And he said to them, "Oh, how foolish you are! How slow of heart to believe all that the prophets spoke! Was it not necessary that the Messiah should suffer these things and enter into his glory?" Then beginning with Moses and all the prophets, he interpreted to them what referred to him in all the scriptures. As they approached the village to which they were going, he gave the impression that he was going on farther. But they urged him, "Stay with us, for it is nearly evening and the day is almost over." So he went in to stay with them. And it happened that, while he was with them at table, he took bread, said the blessing, broke it, and gave it to them. With that their eyes were opened and they recognized him, but he vanished from their sight. Then they said to each other, "Were not our hearts burning [within us] while he spoke to us on the way and opened the scriptures to us?"

Quiet Reflection

How is it possible for parish adult faith formation to open peoples' hearts and minds to the truth of God?

Leader: Let us pray for those who walk with older adults.
All: That their hearts may burn within them.

Leader: Let us pray for those who walk with the young adults.
All: That their hearts may burn within them.

Leader: Let us pray for those who walk with families by word, witness, and action.
All: That their hearts may burn within them.

Leader: Let us pray for those who walk with adults who suffer mentally, physically, or spiritually.
All: That their hearts may burn within them.

Leader: Please add your own intentions.
(moment of silence)
All: That their hearts may burn within them.

Leader: Let us pray together.
All: God, grant us the courage to become true disciples of Jesus.
Disciples who speak that truth which confronts injustice,
rejoices in your mercy,
and burns with a desire to live according to your word.
Amen.

Introduction (20 minutes)

Read the introduction to the OHWB plan (nos. 1-24). In a small group of three people discuss two or three statements that caught your attention as you read the introduction.

Personal Experience (20 minutes)

> Adult faith formation, by which people consciously grow in the life of Christ through experience, reflection, prayer, and study, must be "the *central task* in [this] catechetical enterprise" . . . (OHWB, no. 5)

Think about your own experience of faith formation in adulthood. In the space provided, list one or two of your best experiences of faith formation. Think back upon these experiences and, if possible, record any of the insights or learning that you took away with you. In groups of three, take turns sharing these memories.

Experiences:

_____

_____

_____

Insights:

_____

_____

_____

If possible, name any of the circumstances that contributed to making this faith formation experience a good one.

Circumstances:

_____

_____

_____

Signs of the Times (30 minutes)

Conversion is a lifelong process that leads us to realize the centrality of Christ in our lives. It is dependent on the gifts of the Holy Spirit and, for that reason, both prayer and study play important parts in the conversion process:

> We live in a diverse multicultural society that offers us a rich experience of how the faith is lived, expressed, and celebrated in our own time. We see in this society a widespread spiritual hunger—a quest for meaning and for a deeply personal experience of God and community. . . . Today that Spirit is awakening a new evangelization and a new apologetics. (OHWB, nos. 26 and 28)

- Read the sections of the OHWB plan subtitled "Opportunities and Potential" and "Challenges and Concerns" (nos. 26-37).
- In the space provided, create your own list of various challenges and opportunities for adult faith formation in your parish. Use examples from the OHWB plan as a guide, but don't feel limited by them.

- Gather in groups of five (if in diocesan setting, gather in parish groups) and compare your individual lists. Create a group list of challenges and opportunities to post for all groups to view during the break.

Your Parish's Adult Faith Formation Efforts

Challenges:

Opportunities:

Break (10 minutes)

Fostering Mature Faith (30 minutes)

In a small group of three to five people, spend a few minutes trying to describe adult faith, distinguishing it from children's faith.

Quoting the Church's *General Directory for Catechesis*, the OHWB plan states that a mature adult faith is "a living, explicit, and fruitful . . . faith" (no. 49). To understand what the Church means, complete the following exercise.

Each small group should be assigned one of the three characteristics of mature faith. The group may read about their assigned characteristic in nos. 50-63 of the OHWB plan. Use the following outline to suggest a simple definition for the characteristic, and describe what the parish is doing or could do to nurture an adult faith that is living, explicit, and fruitful. If time allows, small groups should share their insights with the whole group.

1)   Living faith is . . .

_____

_____

_____

Our parish is (or could be) nurturing *living faith* by . . .

_____

_____

_____

2)   Explicit faith is . . .

_____

_____

_____

Our parish is (or could be) nurturing *explicit faith* by . . .

_____

_____

_____

3)   Fruitful faith is . . .

_____

_____

_____

Our parish is (or could be) nurturing *fruitful faith* by . . .

_____

_____

_____

Goals and Principles (30 minutes)

Read the explanation of the three major goals of adult faith formation (OHWB, nos. 67-73). Then use the following exercise to individually assess your parish's implementation of the thirteen principles for adult faith formation (nos. 74-87).

Principles for Adult Faith Formation: A Quick Assessment of Your Parish

Circle the principles for which your parish makes a strong effort.

General Principles for Adult Faith Formation (OHWB, nos. 75-77)

1. Plan adult faith formation to serve "the glory of God, the building of the Kingdom, and the good of the Church."
2. Orient adult Christian learning toward adult Christian living.
3. Strengthen the role and mission of the family in Church and society.

Principles for Planning Adult Faith Formation (OHWB, nos. 78-80)

4. Give adult faith formation the best of our pastoral resources and energies.
5. Make adult faith formation essential and integral to the pastoral plan of the parish.
6. Design adult faith formation opportunities to serve the needs and interests of the entire faith community.

Principles for Conducting Adult Faith Formation (OHWB, nos. 81-83)

7. Use the catechumenate as an inspiring model for all catechesis.
8. Respect the different learning styles and needs of participants, treating adults like adults, respecting their experience, and actively involving them in the learning process.
9. Engage adults actively in the actual life and ministry of the Christian community.

Principles for Inculturating Adult Faith Formation (OHWB, nos. 84-87)

10. "Bring the power of the Gospel into the very heart of culture and cultures."
11. Let the gifts of culture enrich the life of the Church.
12. Involve the whole people of God in inculturating the faith.
13. Let adult faith formation programs be centers of service and inculturation.

In a small group take turns describing a strong effort that you think your parish makes that's related to any one of these principles. Or: If anyone in your group is familiar with the Rite of Christian Initiation of Adults (RCIA), focus on principle 7 above and discuss how the catechumenate (RCIA process) could serve as a model for parish adult formation efforts.

Closing Prayer (10 minutes)

Leader: Lord, you called me before I was born.
All: From my mother's womb you pronounced my name.

Leader: Blessed are you, O God.
All: Ever blessed be your most glorious name.

Leader: May your glory fill all the earth.
All: Amen, amen.

Reader: A reading from the Second Letter to Timothy (3:14–4:5):

But you, remain faithful to what you have learned and believed, because you know from whom you learned it and that from your infancy you have known [the] sacred scriptures, which are capable of giving you wisdom for salvation through faith in Christ Jesus. All scripture is inspired by God and is useful for teaching, for refutation, for correction, and for training in righteousness, so that one who belongs to God may be competent, equipped for every good work.

I charge you in the presence of God and of Christ Jesus, who will judge the living and the dead, and by his appearing and his kingly power: proclaim the word; be persistent whether it is convenient or inconvenient; convince, reprimand, encourage through all patience and teaching. For the time will come when people will not tolerate sound doctrine but, following their own desires and insatiable curiosity, will accumulate teachers and will stop listening to the truth and will be diverted to myths. But you, be self-possessed in all circumstances; put up with hardship; perform the work of an evangelist; fulfill your ministry.

Leader: Let us pray:

Lord, we see the reflection of you and your goodness in ourselves
and we thank you for the talents present in this group.
We are grateful for our gifts.
We humbly ask that you help us to use our gifts wisely
and for your glory.

We ask this through your Son Jesus and his Spirit,
who always remains with us.

All: Amen.

SESSION TWO
THE WHAT AND HOW OF ADULT FAITH FORMATION

Objectives

At the conclusion of Session Two, the participants will have

- Identified the content areas of adult faith formation envisioned in *Our Hearts Were Burning Within Us: A Pastoral Plan for Adult Faith Formation in the United States* (hereafter OHWB)
- Discerned which content areas need concentration within their parish settings
- Explored various concrete approaches for adult faith formation
- Analyzed which approaches have worked before in their parishes
- Suggested various approaches for adult faith formation that might be used in their parishes in the future

Opening Prayer (10 minutes)

Leader: Come, Holy Spirit, fill the hearts of your faithful. Inspire us with wisdom and creativity. Ignite our hearts to burn with dedication as we begin our work.

Reader 1:   "In the first place, it is intended to stress that at the heart of catechesis we find, in essence, a Person, the Person of Jesus of Nazareth. . . . Accordingly, the definitive aim of catechesis is to put people not only in touch but in communion, in intimacy, with Jesus Christ: only he can lead us to the love of the Father in the Spirit and make us share in the life of the Holy Trinity." (*Catechesi Tradendae: On Catechesis in Our Time*, no. 5)

(brief pause)

All: Lord, give us the courage to proclaim Jesus as the Way, the Truth, and the Life. (cf. Jn 14:6)

Reader 2:   "The faith of adults, therefore, must be continually enlightened, developed and protected, so that it may acquire that Christian wisdom which gives sense, unity, and hope to the many experiences of personal, social, and spiritual life." (*General Directory for Catechesis*, no. 173)

(brief pause)

All: Lord, give us the courage to embrace a faith that is living, explicit, and fruitful.

Reader 3:   "Neither catechesis nor evangelization is possible without the action of God working through his Spirit. In catechetical praxis neither the most advanced pedagogical techniques nor the most talented catechist can ever replace the silent and unseen action of the Holy Spirit." (*General Directory for Catechesis*, no. 288)

(brief pause)

All: Come, Holy Spirit, fill the hearts of your faithful.

Reader 4:   "In catechesis 'Christ, the Incarnate Word and Son of God, . . . is taught—everything else is taught with reference to him—and it is Christ alone who teaches. . . .'" (*Catechism of the Catholic Church*, no. 427, citing *Catechesi Tradendae: On Catechesis in Our Time*, no. 6)

Therefore when we teach, we do so as the ambassadors of Jesus. Jesus teaches with our lips—our actions. (cf. *Catechism of the Catholic Church*, no. 427, citing *Catechesi Tradendae: On Catechesis in Our Time*, no. 6)

Reader 4:   As we teach let us be mindful of the words of Jesus: "My teaching is not my own but is from the one who sent me." (Jn 7:16)

All: Lord, may your words be on my lips, that I may proclaim your truth.

Reader 5:   "Catechesis is therefore for adults of every age, including the elderly—persons who deserve particular attention in view of their experience and their problems—no less than for children, adolescents and the young. We should also mention migrants, those who are by-passed by modern developments, those who live in areas of large cities which are often without churches, buildings and suitable organization, and other such groups." (*Catechesi Tradendae: On Catechesis in Our Time*, no. 45)

(brief pause)

All: Lord, help us to minister to the needs of adults of every age and circumstance.

Reader 6:   Luke 24:13-32: The Appearance on the Road to Emmaus (see page 9)

Intercessions: (spontaneous)

All: Lord, give us the courage to embrace a faith that is living, explicit, and fruitful. Help us to build communities that are faithful to your word, courageous in their proclamation of your truth, and joyous in their celebration of the many blessings that you bestow. (cf. OHWB, nos. 49, 67)

Current Parish Efforts (5 minutes)
Take fifteen minutes to complete Charts 1 and 2 by yourself.

Chart 1

Think back over the last three years. List as many adult faith or daily life issues that your parish has discussed, studied, or explored. (Take 5 minutes to list.)

- _____
  _____
- _____
  _____
- _____
  _____
- _____
  _____
- _____
  _____
- _____
  _____
- _____
  _____
- _____
  _____
- _____
  _____
- _____
  _____
- _____
  _____
- _____
  _____

Questions and Concerns About Life and Faith (35 minutes)

Chart 2
What questions or concerns about life and faith might people in the following age ranges have? List up to four questions or concerns for each age range. (Take 10 minutes.)

YOUNG ADULTS: (ages 19-35)	
MIDDLE-AGE ADULTS: (ages 35-60)	
OLDER ADULTS: (ages 60 and older)	

After completing Charts 1 and 2, focus on Chart 2. In a group of three to five people, share your thoughts regarding the questions and concerns that you believe are on the minds of people in the three age ranges listed in Chart 2. (Take 25 minutes.)

Six Content Areas (20 minutes)

> Sacred Scripture provides the starting point for reflecting on the faith, while the *Catechism of the Catholic Church* serves as the "reference for the authentic presentation of the content of the faith." Use of Scripture and the Catechism—including the sources from which it draws, those to which it refers, and other catechetical resources based on and consonant with it—will help adults grasp the content of the faith and its practical application in Christian living. (OHWB, no. 88)
>
> The gift of the *Catechism of the Catholic Church* is an indispensable resource in our time for helping adults become stronger in their relationship with God and grow in their knowledge of the faith. (OHWB, no. 31)

Other approved, authorized, and authentic Catholic texts can serve as resources for particular content areas, as appropriate. Diocesan offices should serve as resources to consult in your planning.

Working with Chart 3

Working in a small group, attempt to redistribute items from the Chart 2 lists of life and faith concerns into the six content areas of Chart 3 (see page 22). If something does not seem to fit into one of these content areas, use the extra spaces in Chart 3 to create additional content areas.

After completing Chart 3, discuss how this chart might be helpful as you organize your diocesan or parish adult faith formation efforts.

Chart 3

Six Content Areas of Adult Faith Formation

Knowledge of the Faith (Doctrine, Teaching, Scripture)	Liturgical Life (Worship, Sacraments)	Moral Formation (Morality, Justice, Lifestyle)

Prayer (Devotion, Contemplation, Retreats)	Communal Life (Strengthening Relationships)	Missionary Spirit (Living and Spreading the Good News)

Place additional content areas here if needed:

Break (10 minutes)

Further Exploration (20 minutes)

> Knowledge of the faith (*fides quae*) is required by adherence to the faith (*fides qua*). Even in the human order the love which one person has for another causes that person to wish to know the other all the more. Catechesis, must, therefore, lead to "the gradual grasping of the whole truth about the divine plan," by introducing the disciples of Jesus to a knowledge of Tradition and of Scripture, which is "the sublime science of Christ." By deepening knowledge of the faith, catechesis nourishes not only the life of faith but equips it to explain itself to the world. (*General Directory for Catechesis*, no. 85)

The *General Directory for Catechesis* (in Part Two, Chapter I) gives norms and criteria for presenting the gospel message in catechesis and (in Part Two, Chapter 2) examines the content of the faith as it is presented in the *Catechism of the Catholic Church*, which is the doctrinal point of reference for all catechesis.

(Review Chart 4 on page 24 before you complete this assessment.)

Working individually, assess the strength of your parish's efforts in each of the six content areas of adult faith formation. Refer to the detailed chart on the next page for an overview. Take your time in reviewing the content suggestions found in Chart 4 before you complete this page.

1. Knowledge of the Faith:
   - ☐ Strong parish effort
   - ☐ Moderate parish effort
   - ☐ Weak parish effort

2. Liturgical Life:
   - ☐ Strong parish effort
   - ☐ Moderate parish effort
   - ☐ Weak parish effort

3. Moral Formation:
   - ☐ Strong parish effort
   - ☐ Moderate parish effort
   - ☐ Weak parish effort

4. Prayer:
   - ☐ Strong parish effort
   - ☐ Moderate parish effort
   - ☐ Weak parish effort

5. Communal Life:
   - ☐ Strong parish effort
   - ☐ Moderate parish effort
   - ☐ Weak parish effort

6. Missionary Spirit:
   - ☐ Strong parish effort
   - ☐ Moderate parish effort
   - ☐ Weak parish effort

Chart 4		
Six Dimensions of Adult Faith Formation Content (cf. OHWB, nos. 88-96)		
Knowledge of the Faith (See the *Catechism*, nos. 26-1065; *General Directory for Catechesis*, nos. 84-85, 87.)	**Liturgical Life** (See the *Catechism*, nos. 1066-1690; *General Directory for Catechesis*, nos. 84-85, 87.)	**Moral Formation** (See the *Catechism*, nos. 1691-2557; *General Directory for Catechesis*, nos. 84-85, 87.)
• Bring people to know, love, and obey *Jesus Christ* as the definitive aim of all catechesis. • Explore the *Scriptures* so that adults may be hearers and doers of the word. • Become familiar with the *great teachings of Christianity* (its creeds and doctrines) and their place in the priority of truths—for example, "the mystery of God and the Trinity, Christ, the Church, the sacraments, human life and ethical principles, and other contemporary themes in religion and morality." • Study the Church's teaching on the *dignity of the human person* in its social doctrine, including its respect-life teaching. • Learn the richness of the *Church's tradition* and understand *church history*. • Develop the *philosophical and theological foundations of the faith.* • Learn the meaning and practical relevance of *current church teachings* as presented by the pope, diocesan bishop, Vatican congregations, and the National Conference of Catholic Bishops.	• Understand, live, and bear witness to the *suffering, death, and resurrection of Jesus,* celebrated and communicated through the *sacramental life of the Church.* • Understand *church doctrine on the eucharist* and the *other sacraments.* • Acquire the spirituality, skills, and habits of *full, conscious, and active participation in the liturgy,* especially the eucharistic liturgy. • Value the dignity and responsibility of our baptism. • Understand the roles of the laity and ordained in liturgical celebrations and Christian mission. • Understand and participate in the Church's daily prayer, the Liturgy of the Hours; and learn to pray the psalms, "an essential and permanent element of the prayer of the Church."	• Understand how the "entire Law of the Gospel is contained in the '*new commandment*' of Jesus, to love one another as he has loved us." • Study the *Ten Commandments, the Beatitudes,* and the moral teachings of the Church, and live in accord with them. • Understand the *dignity, destiny, freedom, and responsibility* of the human person. • Understand the meaning and nature of sin and the power of God's grace to overcome it. • Learn how to acquire and follow a *well-formed conscience.* • Recognize, defend, and live by the truth of *objective moral norms* as taught by the Church's magisterium in its moral and social teaching. • Promote a thorough catechesis on *the Gospel of life* so that *respect for life* from conception until natural death is honored in personal behavior, in public policy, and in the expressed values and attitudes of our society. • Live a *lifestyle reflecting scriptural values.*
Prayer (See the *Catechism*, nos. 2558-2865; *General Directory for Catechesis*, nos. 84-85, 87.)	**Communal Life** (See the *Catechism*, nos. 811-870; *General Directory for Catechesis*, nos. 84, 86, 87.)	**Missionary Spirit** (See the *General Directory for Catechesis*, nos. 84, 86, 87.)
• Become familiar with the diverse *forms and expressions of Christian prayer,* with special attention to "the *Our Father,* the prayer which Jesus taught his disciples and which is the model of all Christian prayer." • Experience and appreciate the richness of the Catholic *tradition* of mysticism and contemplation. • Develop a regular *pattern of personal prayer* and spiritual reflection, recognizing vocal prayer, meditation, and contemplative prayer as basic and fruitful practices in the life of a disciple of Jesus. • Engage in *shared prayer with others,* especially family prayer, as well as at parish meetings and in small communities of faith. • Recognize and encourage practices of *popular piety and devotion* that help believers express and strengthen their faith in Jesus Christ.	• Foster spiritual growth in the community. • Cultivate the human values and Christian virtues that foster growth in *interpersonal relationships* and in *civic responsibility.* • Nurture *marriage and family life.* • Share actively in the life and work of the *parish,* and foster the potential of *small communities* to deepen the faith relationships of members, to strengthen the bonds of communion with the parish, and to serve the Church's mission in society. • Learn the Church's teaching on the *nature and mission of the Church,* including an understanding of the Church's *authority and structures and of the rights and responsibilities of the Christian faithful.* • Support the *ecumenical movement* and promote the unity of God's people as an important dimension of fidelity to the Gospel.	• Cultivate an *evangelizing spirit* among all the faithful. • Respond to *God's call* whether as lay, ordained, or religious. • Motivate and equip the faithful *to speak to others* about the Scriptures, the tradition and teachings of the Church, and about one's own faith journey. • Explore and promote the applications of the Church's *moral and social teaching* in personal, family, professional, cultural, and social life. • Understand the importance of *serving those in need,* promoting the *common good,* and working for the *transformation of society* through personal and social action. • Appreciate the value of *interreligious dialogue* and contacts.

Comparing Notes (10 minutes)

Note the content areas that you rated as moderate or weak in your parish's effort. In your small group, begin to discuss ways in which your parish might strengthen its effort in these areas. (As time may not allow for a thorough discussion, you may want to continue this brainstorming at a later date with members of your parish. Consider setting a date and a time to continue this discussion.)

Approaches to Adult Faith Formation (20 minutes)
(OHWB, nos. 97-112)

"Faith *seeks understanding*": it is intrinsic to faith that a believer desires to know better the One in whom he has put his faith and to understand better what He has revealed; a more penetrating knowledge will in turn call forth a greater faith, increasingly set afire by love. . . . In the words of St. Augustine, "I believe, in order to understand; and I understand, the better to believe." (*Catechism of the Catholic Church,* no. 158)

Review Chart 5 on the next page, which lists various examples of approaches to adult faith formation.

Take a moment to add to the examples under each of the five approaches.

Now circle the specific approaches to adult faith formation that you would like to see your parish use in the coming year.

In a small group, take turns naming an approach to adult faith formation that each member would like to see taken by their parish. Describe the benefits of that particular approach.

Thinking Differently (20 minutes)

Parish "programs" are not the only settings in which adult faith formation occurs. In your small group, brainstorm about the following:

• Ways other than "programs" that adult faith formation either does or could occur

• Ways to support the adult faith formation of the independent learner who is not likely to participate in a parish "program"

Chart 5

Concrete Approaches to Adult Faith Formation
(cf. OHWB, nos. 97–112)

1. Liturgy	2. Family-or Home-Centered Activities	3. Small Groups	4. Large Groups	5. Individual Activities
a. Weekly eucharist • Hospitality • Physical environment • Liturgical ministries • Congregational participation • Music • Homily • Sunday bulletin with educational inserts • Coffee and conversation b. Daily Mass and other communal prayer experiences	a. Learning and spiritual opportunities situated in family settings b. Diocesan newspapers c. Catholic magazines d. Seasonal booklets e. Monthly calendars f. Newsletters g. Periodic mailings h. Pastoral visits i. Family prayer and Scripture sharing j. Home blessings k. Family-to-family ministry l. Videos that promote family faith sharing m. Catholic Internet sites n. Home-based component in programs of catechesis for children and youth	a. Official church movements and associations b. Small intentional learning communities • Small Christian communities • Faith-sharing groups (e.g., peer ministry—groups of divorced, widowed adults; young mothers; young adults; etc.) • Study groups (e.g., Scripture study groups, justice and peace study groups) c. Faith formation processes • Sacramental preparation —Candidates —Parents/families of candidates • RCIA • Spiritual direction	a. Speakers, courses, workshops, mini-courses b. Theology study/discussion c. Intergenerational gatherings d. Potluck suppers with speakers e. Book discussions f. Parish "town meeting" g. Ministry training (e.g., lectors, ushers, parish council, catechists, etc.) h. Formation experiences within every parish meeting (parish council, commissions, etc.) i. Film festivals j. Dinner theater k. Travel l. Mission/renewal m. Retreats (day, evening, or weekend) n. Service involvement and reflection o. Ecumenical activities	a. Materials for personal prayer and study • Print • Audio and video tape • Internet b. Learning through the use of technology • Extension/distance learning videos/tapes • Audio-conferencing • Video-assisted learning • Computer learning • Parish and diocesan web pages and chatrooms • Catholic websites c. Parish lending libraries d. Resources for studying the *Catechism of the Catholic Church* e. Book/tape sales

Closing Prayer (15 minutes)

Leader: Come, Holy Spirit, fill the hearts of your faithful. Inspire us with wisdom and creativity. Ignite our hearts to burn with dedication as we begin our work.

All: Lord, help us to minister to the needs of adults of every age and circumstance.

Reader: Luke 24:13-32: The Appearance on the Road to Emmaus (see page 9)

Leader: Are you hopeful and willing to work to help build up your parish or diocesan adult faith formation efforts? If you can say "yes," describe your hope and enthusiasm to one other person.

(pause for sharing with partners)

All: Lord, give us the courage to embrace a faith that is living, explicit, and fruitful. Help us to build communities that are faithful to your word, courageous in their proclamation of your truth, and joyous in their celebration of the many blessings that you bestow. Amen. (cf. OHWB, nos. 49, 67)

SESSION THREE
ORGANIZING FOR ADULT FAITH FORMATION

Objectives

At the conclusion of Session Three, the participants will have

- Understood the pivotal role of the parish in adult faith formation
- Assessed parish efforts to develop leadership and service for adult faith formation
- Made recommendations that will strengthen parish leadership and service for adult faith formation
- Reviewed ways to contact diocesan offices and staff that support and provide resources for adult faith formation
- Defined the next steps they will need to take in order to move toward implementing *Our Hearts Were Burning Within Us: A Pastoral Plan for Adult Faith Formation in the United States* (hereafter OHWB)

Opening Prayer (10 minutes)

Reader 1:   Lord, as you bring us together
to consider your direction and plan,
provide us with the insight
to recognize your will in all of our efforts,
to realize your guidance in all of our steps, and
to follow your example in all of our works.

Pause for Personal Reflection
What are some of the characteristics of an intentional
and faithful parish adult faith community?

Reader 2:   May we bring to this effort the gifts
you have bestowed on each one of us,
may we affirm the gifts of those who gather with us, and
may we experience greater blessings in our joint endeavors.

Pause for Personal Reflection
What type of gifts are needed if your parish is to have a strong, intentional,
and organized adult faith formation effort?

All: Lord, as we gather, may our vision be clear,
may our work be fruitful, and
may your presence be made known
to all those to whom we minister
in your name.
Amen.

The Pivotal Importance of the Parish (30 minutes)

Read "The Parish *Is* the Curriculum" and "Shaping Parish Culture" in OHWB, nos. 118-123.

In groups of three to five people, discuss what it means to say "the parish *is* the curriculum." (Take 15 minutes.)

Read Appendix I, "Ten Questions to Help Assess and Shape a Parish Faith Community" (page 38). In small groups again, discuss the importance of these questions for efforts to shape the life and mission of a parish. (Take 15 minutes.)

Key Parish Roles of Leadership and Service:
Objective One (15 minutes)

Objective One:
The pastor and other pastoral leaders will demonstrate a clear commitment to the vision and practice of lifelong growth in Christian faith. (OHWB, no. 127)

In groups of three to five people, review Objective One and its description (OHWB, nos. 127-128) and assess your parish's efforts as you focus your discussion on the following indicators. (At a later date, return to nos. 129-130 of the OHWB plan and consider the remaining two indicators.)

Indicator 3: *The parish places adult catechesis at the center of its stated mission and goals, and it promotes the importance of adult faith formation at every opportunity.* (OHWB, no. 131)

☐ Strong parish effort   ☐ Moderate parish effort   ☐ Little or no parish effort

Describe parish efforts:

_____

_____

_____

_____

Recommendations to improve parish efforts:

_____

_____

_____

_____

Indicator 4: *The parish gives adult faith formation a priority in the allocation of financial resources, in providing learning space, and in parish scheduling.* (OHWB, no. 132)

☐ Strong parish effort   ☐ Moderate parish effort   ☐ Little or no parish effort

Describe parish efforts:

_____

_____

_____

_____

Recommendations to improve parish efforts:

_____

_____

_____

_____

Key Parish Roles of Leadership and Service:
Objective Two (20 minutes)

Objective Two:
Each parish will designate an adult faith formation leader—authorized by the pastor and personally involved in ongoing formation—to assume primary responsibility for implementing the ministry of adult faith formation. (OHWB, no. 135)

In groups of three to five people, review Objective Two and its description (OHWB, nos. 135-137).

Discuss the possible value to your parish of designating an adult faith formation leader. (Take 5 minutes.) Or: If your parish has a designated adult faith formation leader, how has such a role been of value to your parish? (Take 5 minutes.)

Review the following two indicators for the adult faith formation leader and assess your parish efforts with regard to each indicator (OHWB, nos. 138-139). (Take 15 minutes.)

Indicator 1: The *parish designates a staff person or qualified lay parishioner as the adult faith formation leader.*

☐ Strong parish effort   ☐ Moderate parish effort   ☐ Little or no parish effort

Describe parish efforts:

_____

_____

_____

Recommendations to improve parish efforts:

_____

_____

_____

Indicator 2: The *leader [of adult faith formation] advocates for the primacy [priority] of adult faith formation in the parish.*

☐ Strong parish effort   ☐ Moderate parish effort   ☐ Little or no parish effort

Describe parish efforts:

_____

_____

_____

Recommendations to improve parish efforts:

_____

_____

_____

If time permits, share some of your recommendations with the large group.

Break (10 minutes)

Key Parish Roles of Leadership and Service:
Objective Three (20 minutes)

Objective Three:
The parish will have a core team of parishioners committed to and responsible for implementing the parish vision and plan for adult faith formation. (OHWB, no. 142)

Review Objective Three regarding the adult faith formation team, and the accompanying indicators, which are listed below (OHWB, nos. 142-148).

> **Indicator 1:** *The parish has a functioning adult faith formation team that is formally recognized in the parish leadership structure.*

> **Indicator 2:** *The parish team, working with the pastor and parish staff, formulates a vision of adult faith formation for the parish.*

> **Indicator 3:** *The team identifies elements of parish life that foster adult growth in faith, assesses their impact, and, if necessary, offers recommendations to enhance their effectiveness.*

> **Indicator 4:** *The team provides a diverse range of quality programming for parish adult faith formation.*

> **Indicator 5:** *The team receives both initial and ongoing formation to prepare it to accomplish its mission effectively.*

The OHWB plan encourages each parish to develop a core team of parishioners who would be responsible for implementing the parish adult faith formation plan. In your small group, discuss the following questions:

- Considering your parish, what are the pros and cons of this "core team" approach?

- Could you imagine developing such an approach in your parish?

- If your parish already has a "core team," how does it measure up when compared to the indicators?

- Aside from a "core team," what other structures or models could assure the implementation of the parish pastoral plan for adult faith formation?

Key Parish Roles of Leadership and Service:
Objective Four (20 minutes)

Objective Four:
Each parish will have access to trained catechists to serve the diverse adult faith formation efforts of the parish or region. (OHWB, no. 149)

> Catechists of adults need to be people of faith with an evangelizing spirit, a zeal for God's kingdom, and a commitment to lifelong formation. They have a sound grasp of Catholic doctrine and theology, an ability to access the various sources of the word of God, and an understanding of how to communicate this knowledge effectively to adults, drawing appropriately upon psychology and the social sciences as needed. They are first people of prayer who recognize their own need to grow in faith. (OHWB, no. 150)

In your small group, discuss the preceding statement and how this description compares with your notion of a "catechist." (Take 5 minutes.)

Comment on the availability in your parish of well-prepared catechists for adult faith formation and funding to assist their continuing formation (OHWB, nos. 152-153). (Take 15 minutes.)

If time permits, consider completing the exercise in Appendix II, "Identifying Diocesan Adult Formation Leaders and Resources" (pages 39-40).

Identifying the Next Steps (30 minutes)
In small groups discuss and list "next step" strategies that would enable you to begin (or continue) to implement the OHWB plan in your parish.

As you plan, consider using "Questions to Get Your Planning Started" (next page).

As you strategize, review the recommendations, opportunities, and challenges that you discussed while working through this guide. Remember, intentional and organized adult faith formation can only be strengthened by your commitment to ongoing implementation of the pastoral plan.

Questions to Get Your Planning Started

General Planning Questions

1. As a result of our study of *Our Hearts Were Burning Within Us: A Pastoral Plan for Adult Faith Formation in the United States,* what issues do we need to address to ensure an intentional and organized adult faith formation effort in our parish?

_____

_____

_____

_____

_____

2. What are the first steps in addressing these issues?

Steps	Timeline

Specific Objectives and Strategies

Think of the following list as objectives to accomplish your goal of quality adult faith formation. Under each objective, suggest one or more strategies to help you accomplish that objective. Add other objectives as needed. (Your diocesan contacts for adult faith formation will be great resources and support as you develop your adult faith formation efforts.)

Objective One: Organize and train a parish team for adult faith formation.

Strategies

_____

_____

_____

_____

_____

_____

Objective Two: Identify and publicize the many existing parish and community opportunities for adult faith formation.

Strategies

_____
_____
_____
_____
_____

Objective Three: Assess the "culture" and needs of the parish.

Strategies

_____
_____
_____
_____
_____

Objective Four: Write a long-range vision and plan.

Strategies

_____
_____
_____
_____
_____

Objective Five: Develop a short-range planning process for the current year.

Strategies

_____
_____
_____
_____
_____

Objective Six: Collaborate with parish leaders and other parish groups.

Strategies

_____
_____
_____
_____
_____

Sending-Forth Prayer (10 minutes)

Leader: The Lord says, "Go, I have appointed you to be a messenger of Good News—to open the eyes of the blind, to set captives free. I have appointed you to be my witness."

All:
(recite
or sing)
Here I am, Lord.
Is it I, Lord?
I have heard you calling in the night.
I will go, Lord,
if you lead me.
I will hold your people in my heart.

Reader 1: And we say, "No Lord, you can't mean me. I am too young. I don't have enough time. I don't speak well. I have too much work. I am afraid. I have other worries."

Reader 2: And then the Lord says, "Go, I have appointed you to be messengers of the Good News. To whomever I send you, you shall go. I will put words into your mouth. And I will be with you every moment, in every struggle and in every joy."

All:
Here I am, Lord.
Is it I, Lord?
I have heard you calling in the night.
I will go, Lord,
if you lead me.
I will hold your people in my heart.

Leader: And the Lord says, "I send you forth to be my hands and feet, my eyes and voice, to a world that needs my life. I give you gifts of grace, gifts to share."

"Go, you are sent. Be my witnesses in this place and in the world, be self-possessed in all circumstances; put up with hardship, perform the work of an evangelist, fulfill your ministry."

All:
Here I am, Lord.
Is it I, Lord?
I have heard you calling in the night.
I will go, Lord,
if you lead me.
I will hold your people in my heart.

Leader: Let us together pray:

May the God of every grace and blessing
Grant us joy and peace.
May we rejoice in God's protection, now and forever.
May God strengthen us and bring our work to completion.
May hope accompany our journey through the days to come.
May God's abiding presence be with us all the days of our life.
May the Lord bless us and keep us.
May God's face shine upon us and be gracious to us.
May God look upon us with kindness and give us his peace.
May God teach us his ways
and lead us to the joys of the kingdom,
now and forever.

May God, our hope and our strength,
Fill us these days with joy in the Holy Spirit.
Let us go in peace to love and serve the Lord.
Amen, amen!

Adapted from "Here I Am, Lord" © 1981, Daniel L. Schutte and New Dawn Music, 5536 NE Hassalo, Portland Oregon 97213. All rights reserved. Used with permission.

Adapted from the Solemn Liturgical Blessings from the English translation of *The Roman Missal*.

APPENDIX I:
TEN QUESTIONS TO HELP ASSESS AND SHAPE
A PARISH FAITH COMMUNITY
(OHWB, no. 122)

1. How are people encouraged to examine their basic assumptions about life and its ultimate meaning?

2. How do they acquire the perspective and skills for an intelligent appropriation of Catholic Christian tradition and an honest, informed assessment of contemporary culture?

3. How is the Christian message lived, communicated, and explored?

4. How do people experience Christian community in family, parish, small groups, and ecumenical encounters?

5. How do they actively participate in liturgical, small group, family, and personal prayer?

6. How are they involved in assessing local needs and discerning pastoral priorities?

7. How is Christian stewardship in parish and society called forth and welcomed?

8. How do they personally serve the "least ones" (Mt 25:45)?

9. How are they involved in shaping public policy and making society more just?

10. How are people learning in the faith already through the ordinary experience of parish life and mission?

APPENDIX II:
IDENTIFYING DIOCESAN ADULT FORMATION LEADERS AND RESOURCES

When time permits, consider completing this additional exercise with the help of your pastor or other resource.

Help is often just around the corner—in a neighboring parish, in your local deanery, or in the diocesan office.

To identify helpful diocesan resources, work with one another (in a small or large group) to fill in as many of the following blanks as possible, and add others if appropriate to your diocese.

In the future, consider investigating and compiling a list of diocesan adult faith formation services, print or media resources, and program offerings.

Diocesan Adult Formation Leaders and Resources

Designated diocesan adult faith formation leader:
Name _____   Office Phone _____

E-mail _____

Leaders or contacts for the following diocesan offices:

Religious Education:
Name _____   Office Phone _____

E-mail _____

Family Ministry:
Name _____   Office Phone _____

E-mail _____

Social Justice:
Name _____   Office Phone _____

E-mail _____

Young Adult Ministry:
Name _____   Office Phone _____

E-mail _____

Multicultural Ministry:

Name _____   Office Phone _____

E-mail _____

Liturgy:

Name _____   Office Phone _____

E-mail _____

Diaconate:

Name _____   Office Phone _____

E-mail _____

Vocations:

Name _____   Office Phone _____

E-mail _____

Evangelization:

Name _____   Office Phone _____

E-mail _____

RCIA:

Name _____   Office Phone _____

E-mail _____

RENEW:

Name _____   Office Phone _____

E-mail _____

Other diocesan staff and offices whose ministry touches on adult faith formation:

Name _____   Office Phone _____

E-mail _____

Name _____   Office Phone _____

E-mail _____

Name _____   Office Phone _____

E-mail _____

Name _____   Office Phone _____

E-mail _____

APPENDIX III:
RESOURCES AND SUPPORT

Some Documents of the Vatican

In *Vatican Council II: Volume 1: The Conciliar and Post Conciliar Documents*, New Revised Edition, Austin Flannery, OP, ed., Northport, N.Y.: Costello Publishing Company, Inc., 1996. USCC pub. no. 44-39:

> Second Vatican Council, *Ad Gentes Divinitus: Decree on the Church's Missionary Activity* (December 7, 1965).

> Second Vatican Council, *Christus Dominus: Decree on the Pastoral Office of Bishops in the Church* (October 28, 1965).

> Second Vatican Council, *Dei Verbum: Dogmatic Constitution on Divine Revelation* (November 18, 1965).

> Second Vatican Council, *Dignitatis Humanae: Declaration on Religious Liberty* (December 7, 1965).

> Second Vatican Council, *Lumen Gentium: Dogmatic Constitution on the Church* (November 21, 1964). USCC pub. no. 000-1.

> Second Vatican Council, *Nostra Aetate: Decree on the Relationship of the Church with Non-Christian Religions* (October 28, 1965).

> Second Vatican Council, *Sacrosanctum Concilium: Constitution on the Sacred Liturgy* (December 4, 1963). USCC pub. no. 303-5.

> Second Vatican Council, *Unitatis Redintegratio: Decree on Ecumenism* (November 21, 1964).

International Council for Catechesis, *Adult Catechesis in the Christian Community: Some Principles and Guidelines*, Washington, D.C.: United States Catholic Conference, 1992. USCC pub. no. 520-8.

John Paul II, Apostolic Exhortation, *Catechesi Tradendae: On Catechesis in Our Time*, Washington, D.C.: United States Catholic Conference, 1979. USCC pub. no. 654-9.

Libreria Editrice Vaticana, *Catechism of the Catholic Church, Second Edition*, Washington, D.C.: United States Catholic Conference, 2000. USCC pub. no. 5-109.

John Paul II, Post-Synodal Apostolic Exhortation, *Christifideles Laici: The Vocation and the Mission of the Lay Faithful in the Church and in the World*, Washington, D.C.: United States Catholic Conference, 1988. USCC pub. no. 274-8.

Paul VI, Apostolic Exhortation, *Evangelii Nuntiandi: On Evangelization in the Modern World*, Washington, D.C.: United States Catholic Conference, 1975. USCC pub. no. 129-6.

John Paul II, Encyclical Letter, *Evangelium Vitae: The Gospel of Life*, Washington, D.C.: United States Catholic Conference, 1995. USCC pub. no. 316-7.

John Paul II, Apostolic Constitution, *Fidei Depositum: On the Publication of the Catechism of the Catholic Church* (1992).

Congregation for the Clergy, *General Directory for Catechesis*, Washington, D.C.: United States Catholic Conference, 1998. USCC pub. no. 5-225.

Congregation for the Doctrine of the Faith, *Libertatis Conscientia: Instruction on Christian Freedom and Liberation* (1986).

Paul VI, Encyclical Letter, *Populorum Progressio: On the Development of Peoples*, Washington, D.C.: United States Catholic Conference, 1967. USCC pub. no. 260-8.

John Paul II, Encyclical Letter, *Redemptor Hominis: The Redeemer of Man*, Washington, D.C.: United States Catholic Conference, 1979. USCC pub. no. 003-6.

John Paul II, Encyclical Letter, *Redemptoris Missio: On the Permanent Validity of the Church's Missionary Mandate*, Washington, D.C.: United States Catholic Conference, 1990. USCC pub. no. 424-4.

John Paul II, Apostolic Exhortation, *Tertio Millennio Adveniente: On the Coming of the Third Millennium*, Washington, D.C.: United States Catholic Conference, 1994. USCC pub. no. 042-7.

John Paul II, Encyclical Letter, *Ut Unum Sint: That They May Be One: On Commitment to Ecumenism*, Washington, D.C.: United States Catholic Conference, 1995. USCC pub. no. 5-050.

John Paul II, Encyclical Letter, *Veritatis Splendor: The Splendor of Truth*, Washington, D.C.: United States Catholic Conference, 1993. USCC pub. no. 679-4.

Some Resources of the National Conference of Catholic Bishops/United States Catholic Conference

Brothers and Sisters to Us: U.S. Bishops' Pastoral Letter on Racism in Our Day, Washington, D.C.: United States Catholic Conference, 1979. USCC pub. no. 653-0.

Called and Gifted for the Third Millennium, Washington, D.C.: United States Catholic Conference, 1995. USCC pub. no. 5-002.

A Family Perspective in Church and Society: A Manual for All Pastoral Leaders, Tenth Anniversary Edition, Washington, D.C.: United States Catholic Conference, 1998. USCC pub. no. 5-273.

Go and Make Disciples: A National Plan and Strategy for Catholic Evangelization in the United States, Washington, D.C.: United States Catholic Conference, 1993. USCC pub. no. 556-9.

Groundwork: Cultivating Adult Religious Education in the Parish, Washington, D.C.: United States Catholic Conference, 1990. USCC pub. no. 393-0.

Guidelines for the Celebration of the Sacraments with Persons with Disabilities, Washington, D.C.: United States Catholic Conference, 1995. USCC pub. no. 5-027.

Guidelines for Doctrinally Sound Catechetical Materials, Washington, D.C.: United States Catholic Conference, 1990. USCC pub. no. 419-8.

The Hispanic Experience in the United States: Pastoral Reflections Using the Catechism of the Catholic Church, Washington, D.C.: United States Catholic Conference, 1996. USCC pub. no. 754-5.

Many Rains Ago: A Historical and Theological Reflection on the Role of the Episcopate in the Evangelization of African American Catholics, Washington, D.C.: United States Catholic Conference, 1990. USCC pub. no. 319-1.

National Pastoral Plan for Hispanic Ministry, Washington, D.C.: United States Catholic Conference, 1987. In *Hispanic Ministry: Three Major Documents*, Washington, D.C.: United States Catholic Conference, 1995. USCC pub. no. 197-0.

Pastoral Statement of U.S. Catholic Bishops on Persons with Disabilities, Washington, D.C.: United States Catholic Conference, 1978. USCC pub. no. 135-0.

Plenty Good Room: The Spirit and Truth of African American Catholic Worship, Washington, D.C.: United States Catholic Conference, 1990. USCC pub. no. 385-X.

Principles for Inculturation of the Catechism of the Catholic Church, Washington, D.C.: United States Catholic Conference, 1994. USCC pub. no. 022-2.

Putting Children and Families First: A Challenge for Our Church, Nation, and World, Washington, D.C.: United States Catholic Conference, 1992. USCC pub. no. 469-4.

Rite of Christian Initiation of Adults: Study Edition, Washington, D.C.: United States Catholic Conference, 1988. USCC pub. no. 214-4.

Serving Life and Faith: Adult Religious Education and the American Catholic Community, Washington, D.C.: United States Catholic Conference, 1986. USCC pub. no. 982-3; Workshop Edition, USCC pub. no. 400-7.

Sharing the Light of Faith, National Catechetical Directory for Catholics of the United States, Washington, D.C.: United States Catholic Conference, 1979. USCC pub. no. 001-X.

Those Who Hear You, Hear Me: A Resource for Bishops and Diocesan Educational/Catechetical Leaders, Washington, D.C.: United States Catholic Conference, 1995. USCC pub. no. 051-6.

Internet Sites

The website of the Vatican: http://www.vatican.va

The website of the United States Conference of Catholic Bishops: http://www.usccb.org

Telephone Numbers

Toll-free number to order resources from USCCB Publishing: 800-235-8722 (In the Washington metropolitan area or outside the United States: 202-722-8716.)

Diocesan Resources

Dioceses often have a number of people and offices that can be helpful in supporting your efforts and suggesting helpful resources for adult faith formation. Fill in the phone numbers of helpful diocesan contacts using Appendix II (pages 39-40) in this leader's guide.

Our Hearts Were Burning Within Us

A Pastoral Plan for Adult Faith Formation
in the United States

Contents

Abbreviations

AA	*Apostolicam Actuositatem: Decree on the Apostolate of Lay People*
ACCC	*Adult Catechesis in the Christian Community: Some Principles and Guidelines*
AN	*Aetatis Novae: A New Era: Pastoral Instruction on Social Communication*
CCC	*Catechism of the Catholic Church*
CCEO	*Code of Canons of the Eastern Churches*
CGTM	*Called and Gifted for the Third Millennium: Reflections of the U.S. Catholic Bishops on the Thirtieth Anniversary of the "Decree on the Apostolate of the Laity" and the Fifteenth Anniversary of "Called and Gifted"*
CIC	*Code of Canon Law*
CT	*Catechesi Tradendae: On Catechesis in Our Time*
DV	*Dei Verbum: Dogmatic Constitution on Divine Revelation*
EN	*Evangelii Nuntiandi: On Evangelization in the Modern World*
GC	*Guide for Catechists*
GCD	*General Catechetical Directory*
GDC	*General Directory for Catechesis*
GS	*Gaudium et Spes: Pastoral Constitution on the Church in the Modern World*
LG	*Lumen Gentium: Dogmatic Constitution on the Church*
NCD	*Sharing the Light of Faith: National Catechetical Directory for Catholics of the United States*
PO	*Presbyterorum Ordinis: Decree on the Ministry and Life of Priests*
RCIA	*Rite of Christian Initiation of Adults*
RM	*Redemptoris Missio: On the Permanent Validity of the Church's Missionary Mandate*

Introduction

"Were not our hearts burning [within us]
while he spoke to us on the way and opened
the scriptures to us?" (LK 24:32)

A RENEWED COMMITMENT TO
ADULT FAITH FORMATION

§ 1 § **W**e are filled with great joy and expectation as the third millennium of Christian history dawns. Before us, in the wonder of God's gracious plan, stretch new opportunities to proclaim the Good News of Jesus to all the world. We are eager to witness and share the word of life about the reign of God faithfully, so that each new generation can hear this word in its own accents and discover Christ as its Savior.

§ 2 § Every disciple of the Lord Jesus shares in this mission. To do their part, adult Catholics must be mature in faith and well equipped to share the Gospel, promoting it in every family circle, in every church gathering, in every place of work, and in every public forum. They must be women and men of prayer whose faith is alive and vital, grounded in a deep commitment to the person and message of Jesus.

§ 3 § The Church's pastoral ministry exists to sustain the work of the Gospel. One way it does this is by nourishing and strengthening lay men and women in their calling and identity as people of faith, as contributors to the life and work of the Church, and as disciples whose mission is to the world. To grow in discipleship throughout life, all believers need and are called to build vibrant parish and diocesan communities of faith and service.

§ 4 § Such communities cannot exist without a strong, complete, and systematic catechesis for all its members. By "complete and systematic" we mean a catechesis that nurtures a profound, lifelong conversion of the whole person and sets forth a comprehensive, contemporary synthesis of the faith,[1] as presented in the *Catechism of the Catholic Church*. This catechesis will help adults to experience the transforming power of grace and to grasp the integrity and beauty of the truths of faith in their harmonious unity and interconnection—a true symphony of faith.[2]

§ 5 § Adult faith formation,[3] by which people consciously grow in the life of Christ through experience, reflection, prayer, and study, must be "the *central task* in [this] catechetical enterprise,"[4] becoming "the axis around which revolves the catechesis of childhood and adolescence as well as that of old age."[5] This can be done specifically through developing in adults a better understanding of and participation in the full sacramental life of the Church.

§ 6 § To make this vision a reality, we, as the Catholic bishops of the United States, call the Church in our country to a renewed commitment to adult faith formation, positioning it at the heart of our catechetical vision and practice. We pledge to support adult faith formation without weakening our commitment to our other essential educational ministries. This pastoral plan guides the implementation of this pledge and commitment.

Jesus, the Model Teacher

§ 7 § The Gospels show how Jesus communicated the Good News. In the familiar story of Emmaus (Lk 24:13-35) we find the model for this pastoral plan.

§ 8 § To be effective ministers of adult faith formation we will first, like Jesus, join people in their daily concerns and walk side by side with them on the pathway of life. We will ask them questions and listen attentively as they speak of their joys, hopes, griefs, and anxieties.

§ 9 § We will share with them the living word of God, which can touch their hearts and minds and unfold the deep meaning of their experience in the light of all that Jesus said and did. We will trust the capacity of prayer and sacrament to open their eyes to the presence and love of Christ. We will invite them to live and share this Good News in the world.

§ 10 § This is the way for us to acknowledge the life-giving power and evangelizing dynamic of encountering Jesus today—just as the two disciples felt their hearts burn within them and returned in haste to Jerusalem to tell their story of meeting Jesus.

§ 11 § Why were their hearts burning? They were burning because in Jesus the disciples caught a glimpse into the heart of God and found their world made new. They saw for an instant the full scope of the Father's loving plan and its high point in Christ's death and resurrection. In that perspective, the pathway of their lives opened from confusion and despair into conviction and hope, and they began to grasp the height and depth of God's mysterious love. What a profound learning experience that must have been!

§ 12 § The passage offers us a model for our ministry and shows the need we all have for ongoing formation in faith. For in it we see two adult disciples who, encountering the risen Lord, grow stronger in love, knowledge, commitment, and zeal. As then, today, "Those who are already disciples of Jesus Christ . . . [need] to be constantly nourished by the word of God so that they may grow in their Christian life."[6]

§ 13 § Such lifelong formation is always needed and must be a priority in the Church's catechetical ministry; moreover, it must "be considered the chief form of catechesis. All the other forms, which are indeed always necessary, are in some way oriented to it."[7]

§ 14 § We are well aware that placing ongoing adult faith formation at the forefront of our catechetical planning and activity will mean real change in emphasis and priorities. In refocusing our catechetical priorities, we will all need to discover new ways of thinking and acting that will vigorously renew the faith and strengthen the missionary dynamism of the Church. Although the task may seem daunting, we need look back no further than the implementation of the Rite of Christian Initiation of Adults twenty years ago to find a model for success. Today, most parishes participate in the catechumenal process, which has brought the Church in the United States great benefit. We seek similar fruits from adult faith formation.

§ 15 § As bishops, we will walk this journey of discovery with you. We write now to offer encouragement and to guide the reorientation of ministerial priorities and practices that we know this plan entails. At the same time, we rely upon your pastoral creativity and dedication to implement the plan effectively. We must go forward firmly rooted in prayer, open to the mystery of God's love, and in touch with the realities of the world. Our dedication and efforts, then, will bear fruit in God's way and time restoring all things in Christ.

Introducing the Plan

§ 16 § This plan builds upon the work already being done by the Catholic community in adult faith formation. The catechumenate is a blessing for those becoming Catholic and for the entire faith community. Renewal programs touch the lives of millions of adult Catholics. Countless Scripture study groups meet regularly to share the word of God and apply it to their lives. Faith-sharing communities are taking root and flourishing around the country. Lay ministry and catechist formation programs each year form tens of thousands of committed adults for service to the Church's mission to proclaim God's reign. Catholic universities and colleges welcome adults into a variety of programs designed to foster their personal growth and to help them develop ministerial skills. Catholic schools and parish religious education programs have enriched the faith of adults who are parents and catechists. Parents in sacrament preparation programs grow in their appreciation of the sacraments and learn to share their faith with their children. Catholic media outlets and publishing companies provide a consistent stream of resources that promote spiritual growth. We offer heartfelt thanks to all who have contributed so generously to these and similar efforts of evangelization and catechesis.

§ 17 § Building on the efforts that have taken place, we seek with this plan to make ongoing faith formation more available, attractive, and effective for all adult Catholics.

- We seek to form *parishes* that are vitally alive in faith. These communities will provide a parish climate and an array of activities and resources designed to help adults more fully understand and live their faith.
- We seek to form *adults* who actively cultivate a lively baptismal and eucharistic spirituality with a powerful sense of mission and apostolate. Nourished by word, sacrament, and communal life, they will witness and share the Gospel in their homes, neighborhoods, places of work, and centers of culture.

§ 18 § This plan for adult faith formation takes its place among other initiatives we have offered in recent years. We addressed today's needs for youth ministry and catechesis in *Renewing the Vision* and for young adult ministry in *Sons and Daughters of the Light*. Some other statements clearly related to this present plan include our national plan for evangelization, *Go and Make Disciples*; our reflections on the social mission of the parish, *Communities of Salt and Light*; our statement on the laity, *Called and Gifted for the Third Millennium*; our synthesis of social doctrine in *Sharing Catholic Social Teaching*; and our letter *In Support of Catholic Elementary and Secondary Schools*. Taken together, these documents offer a body of teaching and a wide-ranging and mutually reinforcing agenda for mission and renewal in the Church in our country. We are convinced that effective adult faith formation will make our efforts in all these initiatives more fruitful.

§ 19 § The plan contains four parts. Fidelity to the Gospel means engagement with the world, and so we begin in Part I with a look at some of the concrete challenges and opportunities that we face. In Part II we describe key elements of mature faith. In Part III we identify three key goals to seek, a number of reliable principles to employ, six content areas to address, and several approaches to follow in providing sound and diversified adult faith formation. In Part IV we focus on the parish as the locus of adult faith formation ministry and identify critical roles of parish leadership and diocesan support.

The Audience for This Plan

§ 20 § We write this plan to all our collaborators who share with us leadership and responsibility for adult faith formation in parishes, dioceses, and other pastoral settings.

§ 21 § We write especially for *parish leaders*:
- Pastors who bear primary responsibility for catechetical formation in their parishes[8]
- Parish adult faith formation leaders, both professional staff and active parishioners
- Directors of liturgy and music
- Other members of parish staffs—clergy, religious, and laity—who share directly or indirectly in responsibility for formation
- All parish faith formation ministers who serve in any role or setting (e.g., as catechists, education team members, RCIA ministers, Scripture study facilitators, sacramental preparation leaders, ministry trainers, small church community leaders or facilitators)
- Administrators and teachers in Catholic schools who have the opportunity to nurture faith in many different settings—whether in the students, in their parents, in themselves, or in their colleagues

§ 22 § We write for *diocesan leaders*:
- Ourselves as bishops, teachers of the faith who bear chief responsibility for "the overall direction of catechesis" in our dioceses[9]
- Our diocesan staffs charged specifically to care for adult faith formation and all their colleagues in diocesan ministry whose work also nurtures adult faith at different stages in the process[10]
- Other diocesan staff members who work with adults in their ministry (e.g., campus ministry, diocesan newspapers, ecumenical and interfaith affairs, evangelization, family life, hospitals or health care ministry, communications, stewardship, youth and young adult ministry, etc.)

§ 23 § We write for those in other *pastoral ministry settings*—such as seminaries, houses of religious formation, colleges and universities, social service agencies, hospitals, nursing homes, prisons, migrant worker camps, pro-life agencies, retreat houses, monasteries—and for those who work in publishing and communications. If you work with adults, you have the opportunity to help them grow in faith. We offer the vision and principles of this plan to guide and encourage you in this essential ministry.

A Time for Awakening

§ 24 § We intend the vision, initiatives, and timeline of this plan to awaken throughout the Church in our country *a passion for renewal in the ministry of adult faith formation*. Through fervent prayer and pastoral work—and relying on the grace of the Holy Spirit—our efforts together will help the whole Catholic people advance in authentic discipleship and fulfill their baptismal call and mission to grow to the full maturity of Christ (cf. Eph 4:13).

I.
A New Focus on Adult Faith Formation

*"I tell you, look up and see the fields
ripe for the harvest."* (JN 4:35)

§ 25 § **A**t all times and in every age, the Church faces unique opportunities and challenges as it proclaims the Good News of God's reign. Today is no exception. We offer below a brief overview of some of the opportunities and challenges we see today. This is the context in which adult faith formation must become our chief catechetical priority.

OPPORTUNITIES AND POTENTIAL

§ 26 § We live in a diverse multicultural society that offers us a rich experience of how the faith is lived, expressed, and celebrated in our own time. We see in this society a widespread spiritual hunger—a quest for meaning and for a deeply personal experience of God and of community. This hunger helps explain the widespread interest today in new religious movements and in New Age spirituality. In this we see opportunity, for "God is opening before the Church the horizons of a humanity more fully prepared for the sowing of the Gospel."[11] People are ready to gather in groups to read the Scriptures, study the teachings of the Church, and talk about the importance of Christ in their lives. They seek out these opportunities wherever they can find them, whether in their own parishes, in ecclesial movements or associations, in small communities of faith, or with people of other Christian traditions.

§ 27 § The world is being reshaped by technology. Not only are computers transforming the way we live and work, they enable many adults to pursue lifelong learning to keep pace with the rapidly changing workplace. Communication technology has also made the world smaller through e-mail, global networks, and increased contacts with other cultures. This globalization of society increases our awareness of and interdependence with other peoples and societies. Adults are responding to these changes by self-directed learning, on-the-job training, and enrolling in continuing education courses in large numbers.

§ 28 § Throughout the centuries the Spirit has guided the Church so that the word would be spread to each generation. Today that Spirit is awakening a new evangelization and a new apologetics. This dynamic movement needs our fullest possible collaboration, so that the Good News of the kingdom of God and the person of Jesus may touch the hearts and minds of all who search for fullness of life. Pope John Paul II's encyclical *Redemptoris Missio* and our own national plan for evangelization, *Go and Make Disciples,* call for such efforts, and their success will require adult believers who are eager and articulate in sharing a faith they understand, embrace, and live.

§ 29 § We are entering a period of new vitality for the Church, a period in which adult Catholic laity will play a pivotal leadership role in fulfilling the Christian mission of evangelizing and transforming society. For adults to fulfill their roles in this new era of the Church, their faith formation must be lifelong, just as they must continue to learn to keep up in the changing world.

§ 30 § Pope John Paul II's apostolic exhortation on the laity, *Christifideles Laici,* and our own reflections in *Called and Gifted for the Third Millennium* envision a laity who are living witnesses to Christ: well-formed in faith, enthusiastic, capable of leadership in the Church and in society, filled with compassion, and working for justice. The power of God's word, regular prayer, a vibrant sacramental life, lay spirituality,[12] the support of the Christian community, and the guidance of the Church's social teaching will enrich and sustain this new era of the laity.

§ 31 § Finally, the gift of the *Catechism of the Catholic Church* is an indispensable resource in our time for helping adults become stronger in their relationship with God and grow in their knowledge of the faith. It should be in regular use: by bishops, priests, and deacons in their preaching and teaching; by those who write and those who publish theological, catechetical, liturgical, and spiritual books and resources; by catechists preparing to work with adults; and by adults themselves in personal and family study and prayer.

CHALLENGES AND CONCERNS

§ 32 § The Church also faces many concerns and challenges. Secularism, materialism, atheism, ethical relativism, religious indifference, and tensions rooted in religious or cultural pluralism are prevalent in society. Many of our contemporaries question the validity of objective moral norms and deny the connection of freedom and truth.

§ 33 § The dignity and sanctity of human life are threatened through the acceptance of contraception, abortion, social injustice, racism, violence of all kinds, discrimination against women, fear of the immigrant or the stranger, threats to the environment, the separation of personal integrity from public life and work, and increasing tolerance for capital punishment and assisted suicide. There is widespread ignorance, indifference, or opposition to the dignity of persons and cultures and to the full range of the Church's moral and social teaching.

§ 34 § Families experience great stress, overwhelmed by the influence of mass media and the economic pressures that keep some families in poverty and almost require both parents to work in order to pay the bills. Parents look to the Church for guidance and help to grow closer as couples, stronger as families, and better able to prepare their children morally and spiritually for life in this complex and challenging society.

§ 35 § Many Catholics seem "lukewarm" in faith (cf. Rev 3:14ff.) or have a limited understanding of what the Church believes, teaches, and lives. Others may know about the gospel message but have not personally experienced the risen Christ. Still others are indifferent to the Church's guidance or see the Church's teaching in a negative light.

§ 36 § For a variety of reasons, people leave the Church. They may seek out or be recruited into non-denominational, evangelical, or fundamentalist churches, or into New Age or other religious movements. Far too often they simply abandon the Christian faith altogether.

§ 37 § We also acknowledge that, together with successes, some of our catechetical efforts have fallen short. It is time to identify and address these shortcomings and build on our strengths so as to forge a more balanced and mature catechetical ministry. Two contemporary resources to help us in this task are the *General Directory for Catechesis* with its pastoral principles and the doctrinal synthesis of the *Catechism*. We must faithfully and creatively adapt both resources to meet both the challenges and the opportunities we face in the United States today.

THE PRIORITY OF ADULT FAITH FORMATION

§ 38 § The challenge of responding to these many needs and opportunities creates a vast pastoral agenda for the Catholic Church. Disciples young and old are called by name to go into the vineyard. In responding to this call, adults "have the greatest responsibilities and the capacity to live the Christian message in its fully developed form."[13] Their formation in faith is essential for the Church to carry out its mandate to proclaim the Good News of Jesus to the world. Effective adult formation is necessary to "equip the holy ones for the work of ministry" (Eph 4:12).

§ 39 § We are convinced that the energy and resources we devote to adult faith formation will strengthen and invigorate all the charisms that adults receive and the activities they undertake, in the Church and in society, to serve the Gospel of Christ and the people of today. Every Church ministry will be energized through a dynamic ministry of adult catechesis.

§ 40 § Adult faith formation also benefits children and youth. An adult community whose faith is well-formed and lively will more effectively pass that faith on to the next generation. Moreover, the witness of adults actively continuing their own formation shows children and youth that growth in faith is lifelong and does not end upon reaching adulthood.[14]

§ 41 § In addition, adult faith formation should serve as the point of reference for catechesis for other age groups. It ought to be "the organizing principle, which gives coherence to the various catechetical programs offered by a particular Church."[15] Maturity of faith is the intent of all catechesis from the earliest years. Thus, all catechesis is geared to a lifelong deepening of faith in Christ. How necessary, then, that the catechetical ministry with adults set an example of the highest quality and vitality.

§ 42 § For such reasons as these, the Church wisely and repeatedly insists that adult faith formation is "essential to who we are and what we do as Church"[16] and must be "situated not at the periphery of the Church's educational mission but at its center."[17]

§ 43 § Yet despite the consistency and clarity of this message, the Catholic community has not yet fully heard and embraced it. While most Catholic parishes place a high priority on the faith formation of children and youth, far fewer treat adult faith formation as a priority. This choice is made in parish staffing decisions, job descriptions, budgets, and parishioner expectations.

§ 44 § Once again, we praise the outstanding efforts that have been made for so many years to provide quality faith formation for children. This task is a sacred trust and a serious responsibility that we must always fulfill with utmost care and dedication. We do not wish to weaken our commitment to this essential ministry in any way. But to teach as Jesus did means calling and equipping all Christians of *every* age and stage of life to fulfill their baptismal call to holiness in family, Church, and society—their mission to evangelize and transform the world into a more caring and just society. Ongoing faith formation is essential to accomplish this mission; it does not end at confirmation or graduation but continues until one's death. Accordingly, we strongly reaffirm that, "without neglecting its commitment to children, catechesis needs to give more attention to adults than it has been accustomed to do."[18] Catholic schools and religious education programs will play a vital role in this plan through the quality faith formation they provide to the parents and families of the children they teach.

II.
Qualities of
Mature Adult Faith and
Discipleship

"By this is my Father glorified, that you bear much fruit and become my disciples." (JN 15:8)

§ 45 § At the heart of all we are and do as the Church is a revelation of great Good News: God, who is love, has made us to enjoy divine life in abundance,[19] to share in the very life of God, a communion with the Holy Trinity together with all the saints in the new creation of God's reign.[20] Faith, which is a gift from God, is our human response to this divine calling: It is a personal adherence to God and assent to his truth.[21] Through searching and growth, conversion of mind and heart, repentance and reform of life, we are led by God to turn from the blindness of sin and to accept God's saving grace, liberating truth, and sustaining love for our lives and for all of creation.

§ 46 § Christian faith is lived in discipleship to Jesus Christ. As disciples, through the power of the Holy Spirit, our lives become increasingly centered on Jesus and the kingdom he proclaims. By opening ourselves to him we find community with all his faith-filled disciples and by their example come to know Jesus more intimately. By following the example of his self-giving love we learn to be Christian disciples in our own time, place, and circumstances.

§ 47 § God's call to conversion and discipleship unfolds in our lives with immeasurable potential for maturing and bearing fruit. The calls to holiness, to community, and to service of God and neighbor are "facets of Christian life that come to full expression only by means of development and growth toward Christian maturity."[22]

§ 48 § This maturity of Christian faith can blossom at any age. We see it in children like Samuel who hear and respond to God's word (cf. 1 Sm 3:1-18). We see it in young people like Mary who ponder and say "yes" to God's call (cf. Lk 1:26-38). We see it in adults and marvel especially at the beauty of faith in those who have persevered in following the Lord over the full course of a lifetime: "They shall bear fruit even in old age, always vigorous and sturdy" (Ps 92:15).

§ 49 § To provide effective adult faith formation requires first of all "the accurate identification of the typical characteristics of Christian adults."[23] What are these characteristics?

What does mature adult faith look like in those who respond generously to God's call? The *General Directory for Catechesis* says that it is "a living, explicit, and fruitful confession of faith."[24] By this, a human being makes a total and free self-commitment to God (DV, no. 7). A full and rich development of these three characteristics is what we aim for in adult catechesis and Christian living.

LIVING FAITH

§ 50 § Faith is both a gift of God and an authentically human response[25]—a recognition of God's call in one's life and a free decision to follow this call by accepting and living the truth of the Gospel. As such, faith is living and active, sharing many of the qualities of living things: it grows and develops over time; it learns from experience; it adapts to changing conditions while maintaining its essential identity; it goes through seasons, some apparently dormant, others fruitful, though wherever faith is present the Holy Spirit is at work in the life of the disciple.

§ 51 § Like all living things, a living faith needs nourishment, which the mature adult disciple finds above all in union with Christ—"the way and the truth and the life" (Jn 14:6). "This life of intimate union with Christ in the Church is maintained by the spiritual helps common to all the faithful, chiefly by active participation in the liturgy."[26] It is also maintained by

- frequent reading of the word of God, sacred writings of our tradition, and the official documents of the Church
- involvement in the community life and mission of the Church
- personal prayer
- participation in the works of justice and service to the poor
- the fulfillment of our human obligations in family and society through the active practice of love for God and neighbor

§ 52 § A living faith is a *searching* faith—it "*seeks understanding.*"[27] Adults need to question, probe, and critically reflect on the meaning of God's revelation in their unique lives in order to grow closer to God. A searching faith leads to deepening conversion.[28] Along the way, it may even experience doubt. Yet the essence of this quality of adult faith is not doubt, but search—a trusting, hopeful, persistent "seeking" or "hunger" for a deeper appropriation of the Gospel and its power to guide, transform, and fulfill our lives.

§ 53 § A living faith is keenly *conscious and aware of the power and hold of sin* in human life (cf. Heb 12:1, Rom 7:14-25). Like the Church, the person of mature faith is "at once holy and always in need of purification."[29] Repentance and renewal, constantly dying to sin and rising by grace to new life—this pattern of the paschal mystery, especially through the sacraments, shapes the whole existence of the mature disciple (cf. Mk 8:34-38, Jn 12:24-26, Rom 6).

§ 54 § Throughout this mortal life, a living faith *longs for the fulfillment of eternal life.* Even though we are now on a pilgrimage, with mature faith we "taste in advance the light of the beatific vision, the goal of our journey here below."[30] This in turn stirs up a greater commitment "to put into action in this world the energies and means received from the Creator to serve justice and peace"[31]—a central mandate of God's reign.

EXPLICIT FAITH

§ 55 § Adult faith is clearly and explicitly rooted in a *personal relationship with Jesus lived in the Christian community*. "The Christian faith is, above all, conversion to Jesus Christ, full and sincere adherence to his person and the decision to walk in his footsteps."[32] Our understanding of the person and the way of Jesus continues to grow by our meditation on the word of God, by prayer and sacrament, by our efforts to follow Jesus' example, and by the sure guidance of the Church's teaching.[33]

§ 56 § Through intimacy with Jesus, a maturing adult faith opens people to a deepening *relationship with* and an "explicit confession of the Trinity."[34] Authentic Christian faith is "radically Trinitarian,"[35] and "the whole Christian life is a communion with each of the divine persons."[36]

§ 57 § Adult faith is explicitly connected to the *life, teaching, and mission of the Church*. As adults mature, a searching faith leads them to examine their lives, their world, and their faith more profoundly. In this quest, they enter into dialogue with the gospel message as professed by the teaching of the Church and lived by the people of God. Through this dialogical process they come not only to know, but to make the faith their own. They acquire that "*ecclesial consciousness*, which is ever mindful of what it means to be members of the Church of Jesus Christ, participants in her mystery of communion and in her dynamism in mission and the apostolate."[37]

§ 58 § Adult faith is confident because it is founded on the word of God[38] and confirmed by the whole Church's supernatural sense of the faith.[39] The adult disciple seeks the clarity and knowledge of faith, so as to find and accept it "with all joy and peace in believing" (Rom 15:13). Out of this conviction come the willingness and ability to witness to the Christian faith whenever possible, to explain it whenever necessary, and to be confidently guided by it always.

§ 59 § "The most valuable gift that the Church can offer to the bewildered and restless world of our time is to form within it Christians who are confirmed in what is essential and who are humbly joyful in their faith."[40] The more this happens, the more it helps us create a climate of "mutual esteem, reverence, and harmony" in the Church and learn to "acknowledge all legitimate diversity. . . . For the ties which unite the faithful together are stronger than those which separate them: let there be unity in what is necessary, freedom in what is doubtful, and charity in everything."[41]

FRUITFUL FAITH

§ 60 § The adult disciple enjoys *the fruits of the Spirit* which are "love, joy, peace, patience, kindness, generosity, faithfulness, gentleness, self-control" (Gal 5:22-23). Mature faith is open to the action and power of God's Spirit and cannot remain idle or unproductive. Where the Spirit is active, faith is fruitful.

§ 61 § Adult faith bears *the fruit of justice and compassion* through active outreach to those in need. Recognizing also the connection of personal sins and social consequences, they pray and work both for personal conversion and for systemic change and social transformation that will serve the common good and, ultimately, the realization of God's reign of justice and peace "on earth as in heaven" (Mt 6:10).

§ 62 § Adult faith bears *the fruit of evangelization*. While fully respecting the religious freedom and choice of others, the adult disciple bears witness in the world to the gift of faith and to the treasure we have found in Jesus and among the community of his disciples. In this process, the witness of the word is essential, but a living witness in the service of love and justice speaks with special power today.

§ 63 § These are some of the characteristics of mature adult faith. But it is essential to remember also that salvation is not the fruit of our innate gifts, our adult competence, or our achievements. Mature faith recognizes that, however great or modest our competence or accomplishments, God's favor is always a gift and a grace. "For by grace you have been saved through faith, and this is not from you; it is the gift of God" (Eph 2:8).

III.
A Plan for Ministry: Goals, Principles, Content, and Approaches for Adult Faith Formation

. . . keeping our eyes fixed on Jesus, the leader and perfecter of faith. (HEB 12:2)

§ 64 § The Church's catechetical mission aims to help the faithful of all ages to grow in both human and Christian maturity,[42] enriching the whole of life with the leaven of the Gospel. Consequently, appropriate goals and content will embrace all the faith dimensions of an adult life—for example, understanding and communicating the faith, skills needed for personal growth, the experience of family life, relationships, public service, and concern for the common good.

§ 65 § Our adult faith formation ministry must engage the particular needs and interests of the adults in each local community. To be faithful and effective it will offer, over time, a comprehensive and systematic presentation and exploration of the core elements of Catholic faith and practice—a complete initiation into a Catholic way of life. It will do so in a way that is accessible to adults and relates to their life experiences, helping them to form a Christian conscience and to live their lives in the world as faithful disciples of Jesus.

§ 66 § This integration of actual life experience, diverse adult learning needs, the study of Scripture, and the teaching of the Church's tradition will create a vibrant learning environment. It will also challenge the creativity of those who establish the direction, plan the content, and provide programs of adult faith formation. Meeting the challenge will be both demanding and rewarding. For guidance, we offer the following goals, principles, content, and approaches.

§ 67 § *Adult Catechesis in the Christian Community*, from the Holy See's International Council for Catechesis, stresses that all catechesis should strive to build adult Christian communities that are strong in faith, clearly proclaim the Gospel, celebrate vibrant and reverent liturgy, and give courageous witness in charity.[43] This document then specifies the following three goals to guide and direct efforts in adult faith formation.

§ 68 § **1) Invite and Enable Ongoing Conversion to Jesus in Holiness of Life.** In response to God's call to holiness, our faith and life as adult disciples are grounded in developing a personal *relationship with Jesus*, "the Holy One of God" (Jn 6:69, Mk 1:24). Accordingly, "'at the heart of catechesis we find, in essence, a Person, the Person of Jesus of Nazareth. . . .' Catechesis aims at putting 'people . . . in communion . . . with Jesus Christ.'"[44]

§ 69 § As its first goal, faith formation helps adults "to acquire an attitude of *conversion to the Lord*."[45] This attitude fosters a baptismal spirituality for adults. It leads them to recognize and repent of sin in their hearts and lives, to seek reconciliation through the sacraments, and to embrace the invitation and challenge of an ever deepening faith in Jesus. It means putting on the mind of Christ, trusting in the Father's love, obeying God's will, seeking holiness of life, and growing in love for others. Deepening personal prayer is a significant means toward growth in holiness in daily life.

§ 70 § **2) Promote and Support Active Membership in the Christian Community.** As adult believers, we learn and live our faith *as active members of the Church*. Our response to God's call to community "cannot remain abstract and unincarnated," but rather, "reveals itself concretely by a visible entry into a community of believers . . . a community which itself is a sign of transformation, a sign of newness of life: it is the Church, the visible sacrament of salvation."[46] People find this community of faith in the parish and diocese, as well as in their families, small church communities, personal relationships, faith-based associations, and in the communion of saints of all times and places.

§ 71 § Accordingly, faith formation helps adults make "a conscious and firm decision to live the gift and choice of faith through *membership in the Christian community*," accepting "coresponsibility for the community's mission and internal life."[47] Adults not only receive the ministries of the Christian community, they also contribute to its life and mission through the generous stewardship of their gifts.

§ 72 § **3) Call and Prepare Adults to Act as Disciples in Mission to the World.** The Church and its adult faithful have *a mission in and to the world*: to share the message of Christ to renew and to transform the social and temporal order. This dual calling to evangelization and justice is integral to the identity of the lay faithful; all are called to it in baptism.

§ 73 § Accordingly, faith formation seeks to help each adult believer become "more willing and able to be a *Christian disciple in the world*."[48] As salt of the earth and light for the world (cf. Mt 5:13-16), adult disciples give witness to God's love and caring will so that, in the power of the Spirit, they renew the face of the earth.

§ 74 § To assist the implementation of these goals, we offer here some basic principles of adult faith formation.

General Principles for Adult Faith Formation

§ 75 § *(1) Plan adult faith formation to serve "the glory of God, the building of the Kingdom, and the good of the Church."*[49] Effective adult faith formation calls us to give God glory through our prayers of praise and the lives we lead. It equips us to be people of salt and light who build up God's kingdom of truth and life, holiness and grace, justice, love, and peace.[50] It leads us to promote the good of the Church, serving its internal life and its dual mission of evangelization and justice.

§ 76 § *(2) Orient adult Christian learning toward adult Christian living.* Effective adult faith formation efforts join faith and life. They help people in practical ways to live their daily lives by the light and power of the Gospel.

§ 77 § *(3) Strengthen the role and mission of the family in Church and society.* Adults are eager for resources, guidance, and support that will help them form a community of faith within their families, grow more deeply in love with their spouses, raise children committed to Jesus and the Church, participate as Catholic families in society, and share together in the life and mission of their parish and the wider Church.[51]

Principles for Planning Adult Faith Formation

§ 78 § *(4) Give adult faith formation the best of our pastoral resources and energies.* Within the whole scope of catechetical ministry, adult catechesis "must be regarded as a preferential option"[52] in planning and programming. When adult catechesis excels, it can then serve effectively as the point of reference and organizing principle for all catechesis.[53]

§ 79 § *(5) Make adult faith formation essential and integral to the pastoral plan of the parish.* Effective adult formation ministry connects with and strengthens all the many ministries and activities of the parish—formational, charitable, devotional, social, administrative. This integration of parish life and ministry helps to form the whole community on its lifelong journey of growth in Christian faith and mission.

§ 80 § *(6) Design adult faith formation opportunities to serve the needs and interests of the entire faith community.* "The Church therefore must maintain an active, listening presence in relation to the world—a kind of presence which both nurtures community and supports people in seeking acceptable solutions to personal and social problems."[54] Start by listening to adults and let the stories of their lives and the hungers of their hearts inspire pastoral care and inform catechetical programming. Reach out to those whom society often neglects.[55]

Principles for Conducting Adult Faith Formation

§ 81 § *(7) Use the catechumenate as an inspiring model for all catechesis.*[56] The baptismal catechumenate provides for an apprenticeship in Christian living and believing. It "seems the most appropriate model" for adult faith formation and, though it cannot be considered the exclusive model, should be encouraged everywhere.[57] Whatever model is used, adult faith formation should always actively challenge participants to get involved with their own faith journey—passive listening is never enough; the goal is always conversion.

§ 82 § *(8) Respect the different learning styles and needs of participants, treating adults like adults, respecting their experience, and actively involving them in the learning process.* Effective adult faith formation "must begin by *accepting adults where they are*"[58] in their faith, their life situations, their experiences, and their preferred learning styles. Our programs and ministries must be in touch with people's real circumstances and concerns. Just as Jesus did with the disciples on the road to Emmaus, we must journey with people, listen to them, share our faith, help them to find in the Good News the answer to their hearts' deepest questions, and prepare them to live as Jesus' disciples.

§ 83 § *(9) Engage adults actively in the actual life and ministry of the Christian community.* "Adults do not grow in faith primarily by learning concepts, but by sharing the life of the Christian community."[59] Not that concepts are irrelevant; they are foundational. But for most people the truths of faith really come alive and bear fruit when tested and put into practice—in soup kitchens, neighborhoods, small groups, workplaces, community organizations, and family homes. Adult catechesis practitioners need to learn to tap the learning potential of these diverse settings of Christian ministry and daily life.

Principles for Inculturating Adult Faith Formation

§ 84 § *(10) "Bring the power of the Gospel into the very heart of culture and cultures."*[60] Sometimes this means discerning with participants which aspects of their culture are compatible with the Gospel and then building adult faith formation efforts on those aspects, incorporating the culture's symbols, traditions, and language. At other times it means discerning cultural elements incompatible with the Gospel and working together to purify and transform them. Both are important; neither should be neglected.

§ 85 § *(11) Let the gifts of culture enrich the life of the Church.* Inculturation is a process of mutual enrichment between the Gospel and culture.[61] While the power of the Gospel transforms and renews each culture that embraces it, the living tradition of each culture gives rise to "original expressions of Christian life, celebration, and thought"[62] that become gifts for the whole Church. Find ways to emphasize the gifts of ethnic and cultural diversity. We all want and deserve to be respected for who we are, with our personal qualities and cultural characteristics recognized as part of God's creative presence in the world.

§ 86 § *(12) Involve the whole people of God in inculturating the faith.* "Inculturation must involve the whole people of God, and not just a few experts, since the people reflect the authentic *'sensus fidei'* which must never be lost sight of."[63] Work directly with people of each racial or ethnic group to find ways to affirm or renew the values expressed in their family traditions, social customs, and popular devotions. Special attention must be paid to those groups that are most easily forgotten: particularly those who are elderly, those who are living with handicapping conditions, those who are alienated from society.

§ 87 § *(13) Let adult faith formation programs be centers of service and inculturation.* Be conscious of those whose racial, linguistic, or ethnic identity may cause them to feel alienated from the local culture or faith community, to experience overt or subtle discrimination, or to be economically disadvantaged. Make every effort to reach out and welcome them, tactfully offering any needed assistance, and incorporating them in the life and activities of the church community as full and valued members.

Six Dimensions

§ 88 § Scripture and tradition form the core content of all adult catechesis, for the Church has always considered them the "supreme rule of faith." Through them we receive "the very word of God," and in them resounds "the voice of the Holy Spirit."[64] Sacred Scripture provides the starting point for reflecting on the faith, while the *Catechism of the Catholic Church* serves as the "reference for the authentic presentation of the content of the faith."[65] Use of Scripture and the *Catechism*—including the sources from which it draws, those to which it refers, and other catechetical resources based on and consonant with it—will help adults grasp the content of the faith and its practical application in Christian living.

§ 89 § The Catholic faith is like a symphony in which the unity of faith finds expression in richly diverse formulations and manifestations.[66] As the *General Directory for Catechesis* states, "The maturation of the Christian life requires that it be cultivated in all its dimensions: knowledge of the faith, liturgical life, moral formation, prayer, belonging to community, missionary spirit. When catechesis omits one of these elements, the Christian faith does not attain full development."[67]

§ 90 § The ongoing development of a living, explicit, and fruitful Christian faith in adulthood requires growth in all six dimensions. Each of them is a fundamental aspect of Christian life and a foundational content area for adult faith formation. The exploration of the six dimensions that follow are presented as content summaries to indicate what adult faith formation programs and opportunities seek to accomplish.

§ 91 § 1) Knowledge of the Faith
(See the Catechism, *nos. 26-1065;* General Directory for Catechesis, *nos. 84-85, 87.)*

- Recognize *communion with Jesus Christ* as the definitive aim of all catechesis.
- Explore the *Scriptures* so that adults may be hearers and doers of the word.
- Become familiar with the *great teachings of Christianity* (its creeds and doctrines) and their place in the hierarchy of truths—for example, "the mystery of God and the Trinity, Christ, the Church, the sacraments, human life and ethical principles, eschatological realities, and other contemporary themes in religion and morality."[68]
- Study the Church's teaching on the *dignity of the human person* in its social doctrine, including its respect-life teaching.
- Learn the richness of the *Church's tradition*, explore the *theological and cultural heritage* in which faith is expressed, and gain perspective on contemporary events and trends through an understanding of *church history.*
- Develop the *philosophical and theological foundations of the faith* and appreciate expressions of *Christian thought and culture.*

- Learn the meaning and practical relevance of *current church teachings* as presented by the pope, diocesan bishop, Vatican congregations, and the National Conference of Catholic Bishops.

§ 92 § 2) Liturgical Life
(See the Catechism, *nos. 1066-1690; General Directory for Catechesis, nos. 84-85, 87.)*

- Understand, live, and bear witness to the *paschal mystery*, celebrated and communicated through the *sacramental life of the Church*.
- Learn and embrace in one's life church *doctrine on the eucharist* and the *other sacraments*.
- Acquire the spirituality, skills, and habits of *full, conscious, and active participation in the liturgy*, especially the eucharistic liturgy.
- Value the dignity of the *baptismal priesthood* and of the *ordained priesthood* and their respective roles in liturgical celebration and Christian mission.
- Appreciate and appropriately participate in the Church's daily prayer, the *Liturgy of the Hours*, and learn to pray the *psalms*, "an essential and permanent element of the prayer of the Church."[69]

§ 93 § 3) Moral Formation
(See the Catechism, *nos. 1691-2557; General Directory for Catechesis, nos. 84-85, 87.)*

- Understand how the "entire Law of the Gospel is contained in the '*new commandment*' of Jesus, to love one another as he has loved us,"[70] and promote each disciple's formation in the life of the risen Christ.
- Study the *Ten Commandments, the Beatitudes*, and the moral catechesis of the apostolic teachings, and live in accord with them.
- Appreciate the *dignity, destiny, freedom, and responsibility* of the human person, together with the reality of *sin* and the power of God's *grace* to overcome it.
- Learn how to acquire and follow a *well-formed conscience* in personal and social life, clarifying current *religious and moral questions* in the light of faith, and cultivating a Christian discernment of the *ethical implications* of developments in the socio-cultural order.
- Recognize, defend, and live by the truth of *objective moral norms* as taught by the Church's magisterium in its moral and social teaching.
- Promote a thorough catechesis on *the Gospel of life* so that *respect for life* from conception until natural death is honored in personal behavior, in public policy, and in the expressed values and attitudes of our society.
- Live a *lifestyle reflecting scriptural values* of holiness, simplicity, and compassion.

§ 94 § 4) Prayer
(See the Catechism, *nos. 2558-2865; General Directory for Catechesis, nos. 84-85, 87.)*

- Become familiar with the diverse *forms and expressions of Christian prayer*, with special attention to "the *Our Father*, the prayer which Jesus taught his disciples and which is the model of all Christian prayer."[71]
- Experience and appreciate the richness of the Catholic *ascetical-mystical tradition* as it has taken form across the centuries in diverse historical and cultural settings.

- Develop a regular *pattern of personal prayer* and spiritual reflection, recognizing vocal prayer, meditation, and contemplative prayer as basic and fruitful practices in the life of a disciple of Jesus.
- Engage in *shared prayer with others*, especially family prayer, as well as at parish meetings and in small communities of faith.
- Recognize and encourage practices of *popular piety and devotion* that help believers express and strengthen their faith in Jesus Christ.

§ 95 § 5) Communal Life
(See the General Directory for Catechesis, *nos. 84, 86-87.)*

- Pursue *personal and spiritual growth* in human and Christian maturity.
- Cultivate the human values and Christian virtues that foster growth in *interpersonal relationships* and in *civic responsibility*.
- Nurture *marriage and family life* to build up the Church of the home.
- Share actively in the life and work of the *parish*, and foster the potential of *small communities* to deepen the faith and relationships of members, to strengthen the bonds of communion with the parish, and to serve the Church's mission in society.
- Learn the Church's teaching on the *nature and mission of the Church*, including an understanding of the Church's *authority* and *structures* and of the *rights and responsibilities of the Christian faithful*.
- Support the *ecumenical movement* and promote the unity of God's people as a constitutive dimension of fidelity to the Gospel.

§ 96 § 6) Missionary Spirit
(See the General Directory for Catechesis, *nos. 84, 86-87.)*

- Cultivate an *evangelizing spirit* among all the faithful as an integral element of their baptismal calling, of the Church's nature and mission, and of a Catholic way of life.
- Respond to *God's call* whether as lay, ordained, or religious, and develop a *personal apostolate* in family, Church, and society.
- Motivate and equip the faithful *to speak to others* about the Scriptures, the tradition and teachings of the Church, and one's own experience of faith.
- Explore and promote the applications of the Church's *moral and social teaching* in personal, family, professional, cultural, and social life.
- Understand the importance of *serving those in need*, promoting the *common good*, and working for the *transformation of society* through personal and social action.
- Appreciate the value of *interreligious dialogue* and contacts, and promote the Church's mission *ad gentes* in the local and universal Church.

CONCRETE APPROACHES

§ 97 § The scope of catechetical content is cognitive, experiential, and behavioral[72] and it requires development in "the threefold dimension of word, memory, and witness (doctrine, celebration, and commitment in life)."[73] This balanced method fosters growth in both the faith *by which* we believe and the faith *in which* we believe. As the *General Directory for Catechesis* says, "this 'Yes' to Jesus Christ, who is the fullness of revelation of the Father, is twofold: a trustful abandonment to God and a loving assent to all that he has revealed to us."[74] It takes place "through formation in doctrine and the experience of Christian living"[75]—both together foster each disciple's growth into the full faith and life of the Gospel. This approach also promotes a natural linkage between the faith we profess and celebrate and the life we live, thus meeting one of the principal challenges of our day.

A Multi-Faceted Approach

§ 98 § Given the broad scope of content, the diverse range of adult interests and responsibilities, and the availability of learning resources, no single approach can meet everyone's needs. Consequently, *a comprehensive, multi-faceted, and coordinated approach* to adult faith formation is necessary. Parish leaders need to provide a *variety* of learning activities and resources to meet the diverse needs of parishioners. Inter-parish cooperation is a developing and important dynamic that can increase learning opportunities for parishioners, especially (but not only) for smaller parishes.

§ 99 § Ongoing faith formation can be "accomplished through a great variety of forms: 'systematic and occasional, individual and community, organized and spontaneous.'"[76] Learn to see and take advantage of every opportunity to help adults appreciate and grow in their faith. The following five approaches can be used in some way in any Catholic community, and are to be adapted as appropriate to parish size and need.

§ 100 § 1) Liturgy

Each Sunday, the majority of our Catholic adults gather as a community of faith to celebrate the eucharist in praise of God, in joyful faith, and in a deepening discipleship with the Lord Jesus. Sunday eucharist remains the center of the Church's life. Indeed, active participation in the liturgy "is the primary and indispensable source from which the faithful are to derive the true Christian spirit"[78] and deepen their conversion to God.

§ 101 § Liturgy fosters this ongoing conversion, uniting us in Christ and with one another, uplifting our spirits in thankful, joyful praise, and renewing our hearts in love for God, turning us to love of neighbor. Each aspect of worship—the homily, the physical environment, hospitality, liturgical ministries, congregational participation, appropriate music, the Sunday bulletin with inclusions—has the potential to foster adult faith, bringing people into a more intimate relationship with Christ and with one another.[79] Daily Mass and other communal prayer experiences provide additional formative opportunities.

§ 102 § 2) Family- or Home-Centered Activities

There may be no place more significant for catechesis than the family. "Family catechesis precedes . . . accompanies and enriches all forms of catechesis"[80]—and this applies in any structure or stage of family life.

§ 103 § Catechetical opportunities situated in family settings foster both adult and family faith growth, while also addressing one of the major reasons adults give for not participating in adult education: time away from their families. Maximize opportunities for adult faith formation to fit into the rhythms of family life and not to pull families apart.

§ 104 § Diocesan newspapers (frequently overlooked for their potential), Catholic magazines, seasonal booklets, monthly calendars, newsletters, periodic mailings, pastoral visits, family prayer and Scripture sharing, home blessings, family-to-family ministry, videos that promote family faith sharing, Catholic websites, and a home-based component in programs of catechesis for children and youth can all provide adults and their families with meaningful faith formation experiences. "The means of social communication are used to complement the established ways of teaching. They also give opportunities for further education to adolescents and adults."[81]

§ 105 § 3) Small Groups

Many Catholic adults already meet regularly in a variety of small groups for encouragement to better live their faith in the world and to build community. In their various forms these groups provide genuine support to people in living their faith in daily life. "As basic units of the parish, they serve to increase the corporate life and mission of the parish by sharing in its life generously with their talents and support."[82]

§ 106 § Small communities are powerful vehicles for adult faith formation, providing opportunities for learning, prayer, mutual support, and the shared experience of Christian living and service to Church and society. Ecclesial movements and associations that are part of the vibrant life of the Church make great contributions here. We welcome this phenomenon as "a sign of the 'Church's vitality,'"[83] and have offered guidelines for authentic small faith community development in *Called and Gifted for the Third Millennium* and in *Communion and Mission*.

§ 107 § 4) Large Groups

Some adults prefer to learn in large group settings. It can be effective and efficient to take advantage of times when adults are already present, as when their children's catechetical sessions are scheduled. Other settings may include lectures, panel presentations and discussions, group service projects, social events (e.g., Lenten suppers) with a prayer or learning component, ecumenical activities during the Week of Prayer for Christian Unity, participation in the March for Life on January 22, and working together to provide housing for low-income families or to build or repair parish facilities. We encourage parishes to provide a variety of regular larger group opportunities for adult faith formation.

§ 108 § 5) Individual Activities

Adults also spend time alone—commuting or traveling, doing yardwork or household chores, keeping a "holy hour," or finding a few minutes in the morning or at night for reflection and prayer. Some adults, especially the sick or homebound, spend much time alone. With the right resources and assistance, this time alone can lead to a growing relationship with Jesus.

§ 109 § Materials for personal prayer, study, and reflection are available in print, on audio or videotape, and on the Internet. We need creative ways to make these items more widely known and easily accessible through the use of media. For example, parish bulletins or diocesan newspapers can publicize books or websites, and parish lending libraries or book/tape sales can provide resources to adults. Parishes and dioceses can develop their own webpages or chat rooms, which people can access at any time to engage in a discussion with other people of faith, or find religious news or information about prayer, the Catholic tradition, or current events.

§ 110 § We encourage all Catholics to spend some time alone with God each day, whether they meditate on Scripture, use printed or memorized prayers, the Liturgy of the Hours, the rosary, meditation and contemplative prayer, or simply dwell in wordless praise in God's loving presence. Even five minutes a day devoted to one's relationship with the Lord can lead to a deepened faith and a more active Christian witness.

Implementing These Approaches

§ 111 § Because of their differences in size and resources, each parish will have to determine its own array of faith formation opportunities from each of the five preceding areas. But the basic principle remains valid in all cases: "the local Church must . . . provide diversified programs of permanent catechesis for Christian adults."[84]

§ 112 § We encourage new and creative initiatives in every Catholic community. But we also encourage making the most of existing parish activities and services. In fact, every aspect and event in parish life can be intentionally fashioned as an occasion for adult faith formation. For example, every parish meeting can begin with a reading of the upcoming Sunday's Gospel, followed by a time of reflection and faith sharing. Being intentional about catechetical opportunities can significantly enhance adult faith formation in every community. Whatever approach is used, each parish needs to consider seriously how it will make the lifelong faith formation of its adult members its chief catechetical concern.

IV.
A Plan for Ministry: Organizing for Adult Faith Formation

*And he gave some as apostles,
others as prophets, others as evangelists,
others as pastors and teachers, to equip the
holy ones for the work of ministry,
for building up the body of Christ,
until we all attain to the unity of faith and
knowledge of the Son of God,
to mature manhood, to the extent of the
full stature of Christ. (EPH 4:11-13)*

§ 113 § **M**aking adult faith formation a vibrant and fruitful reality in parish life will require the support of a solid infrastructure of ministry in local faith communities. In Part IV we identify key elements of this organizational support. We begin with reflections on the *parish*; it is where much adult faith formation takes place, and it is the chief ministerial agent of such formation within and beyond the parish. We then focus on the *people* needed for this ministry, for "the quality of any form of pastoral activity is placed at risk if it does not rely on truly competent and trained personnel."[85]

THE PIVOTAL IMPORTANCE OF THE PARISH

§ 114 § For most Catholics, the parish is their primary experience of the Church. It is where they gather for weekly worship, celebrate their most joyous occasions, and mourn their deepest losses. There they are called to repentance and renewal, finding and celebrating God's forgiveness and reconciliation. Embracing the dying and rising of Jesus in their lives, they are challenged to holiness and strengthened for self-giving love and Christian service.

§ 115 § At the same time, not everyone who seeks to live a Catholic life does so through regular parish membership. We are challenged to find effective ways to walk the journey of life with all Catholics—including those without a strong parish connection—and to enrich that shared journey with the gifts of the faith community. Even as we walk with these non-parish Catholics, we seek ways to bring them back again to active parish life.

§ 116 § The ministerial personnel and infrastructure to meet this challenge will be found chiefly in the parish and diocesan community, as described below. And yet this responsibility belongs fundamentally to the whole parish, which is called to be "a visible place of faith-witness" and "the living and permanent environment for growth in the faith."[86]

§ 117 § The parish, then, provides the place, persons, and means to summon and sustain adults in lifelong conversion of heart, mind, and life. It is, "without doubt, the most important *locus* in which the Christian community is formed and expressed."[87]

§ 118 § 1) The Parish *Is* the Curriculum

While this pastoral plan is concerned primarily with intentional adult faith formation programs, the success of such efforts rests very much on the quality and total fabric of parish life. This includes, for example, "the quality of the liturgies, the extent of shared decision making, the priorities in the parish budget, the degree of commitment to social justice, the quality of the other catechetical programs."[88]

§ 119 § Parishioners' personal involvement in ministry is also formative. They learn as they prepare for ministry and as they engage in it; they learn from those with whom they serve and from those whom they serve; and by their witness, they show others the life-giving power of faith.

§ 120 § The homily holds powerful potential for fostering the faith of adults.[89] It "takes up again the journey of faith put forward by catechesis, and brings it to its natural fulfillment. At the same time, it encourages the Lord's disciples to begin anew each day their spiritual journey in truth, adoration and thanksgiving."[90]

§ 121 § When these various elements of parish life are weak or lacking, formal programs for adults typically do not flourish; when they are vibrant and strong, they create an overall climate of active participation and living faith that can only benefit the parish's intentional formation efforts with adults. Thus, while the parish may *have* an adult faith formation program, it is no less true that the parish *is* an adult faith formation program.

§ 122 § 2) Shaping Parish Culture

To foster this living climate of faith, pastors and those with whom they collaborate in pastoral leadership will want to assess and intentionally shape the culture and procedures of the parish, using questions such as, How are people encouraged to examine their basic assumptions about life and its ultimate meaning? How do they acquire the perspective and skills for an intelligent appropriation of Catholic Christian tradition and an honest, informed assessment of contemporary culture? How is the Christian message lived, communicated, and explored? How do people experience Christian community in family, parish, small groups, and ecumenical encounters? How do they actively participate in liturgical, small group, family, and personal prayer? How are they involved in assessing local needs and discerning pastoral priorities? How is Christian stewardship in parish and society called forth and welcomed? How do they personally serve the "least ones" (Mt 25:45)? How are they involved in shaping public policy and making society more just? In short, how is learning in faith already happening through the ordinary experience of parish life and mission?

§ 123 § A 1990 study of Protestant congregations identified two factors as having the strongest positive influence on the faith maturity and loyalty of adults: *lifelong involvement in Christian education* (during childhood, adolescence, and adulthood) and *lifelong involvement in the life of the Church*.[91] This data is affirmed in the study conducted by James Davidson et al. that stresses the importance of personal attributes, upbringing, life course experiences, and commitment in relationship to one's beliefs and practices.[92] Whatever we can do in Catholic parishes and dioceses to encourage lifelong involvement in church life and faith formation will bear fruit in strengthened Christian community and mission.

KEY PARISH ROLES OF LEADERSHIP AND SERVICE FOR ADULT FAITH FORMATION

§ 124 § To make adult faith formation ministry most effective, certain roles of leadership and corresponding pastoral structures are critical. These roles constitute a ministerial infrastructure that we believe is necessary to sustain a healthy parish practice of adult faith formation.

§ 125 § The following objectives highlight four key roles: (1) the *pastor* and other pastoral leaders; (2) the *adult faith formation leader* who becomes the lead agent in promoting and supporting this ministry in the parish; (3) the *adult faith formation team* who collaborates with the leader in planning and providing learning opportunities; and (4) *catechists of adults*.

§ 126 § While the whole parish is responsible for catechetical ministry, these four leadership roles are critical lead agents. In this section we describe these roles, introduce objectives to be accomplished, and propose indicators to help in assessing attainment of the objectives. Objectives and indicators are based upon successful pastoral practice. They are meant as guides for enhancing and expanding effective adult faith formation, and they can be adapted to local needs and circumstances.

The Pastor and Other Pastoral Leaders

§ 127 § *Objective One:*
> *The pastor and other pastoral leaders will demonstrate a clear commitment to the vision and practice of lifelong growth in Christian faith.*

The pastor bears the pastoral and spiritual responsibility, as reflected in the code of canon law, for catechesis in the parish and for ensuring an authentic presentation of the faith to adults.[93] He personally models mature adult faith and is its principal advocate in the parish.

He sees to it that adults of all ages have opportunities to learn and grow in faith throughout their lives. To equip them for these tasks, seminarians, priests, and deacons are to study catechetical methodology, especially the principles and practices of adult faith formation.[94] "Experience bears out that the quality of catechesis in a community depends very largely on the presence and activity of the priest."[95]

§ 128 § In parishes with additional pastoral staff, the pastor ensures that all staff members promote adult faith formation as a parish priority. In communities without a resident pastor, the pastoral administrator ensures that adult faith formation opportunities are provided.

INDICATORS

- § 129 § *The pastor establishes parish policies and procedures that give priority to the vision and practice of adult faith formation.* Personally, the pastor promotes the vision of mature faith in the normal course of his ministry—through working with the pastoral council and parish committees, in supervision of the parish staff, in his homilies, and by encouraging everyone's active participation in the mission of the parish and in the Church's ministry of the word. In keeping with their charisms and inclinations they are responsible for teaching adults, for priests are "educators of the faith" by virtue of ordination.[96] They assure that the parish budget funds staffing, training, and resourcing for adult faith formation to the fullest extent possible. The pastor charges the adult faith formation leader and team to provide "multiple forms of ongoing education in the faith,"[97] well suited to the diverse needs of the parish. He fosters their work through clear and enthusiastic endorsements of adult faith formation opportunities. He encourages networking and collaboration across parish boundaries and with regional and diocesan initiatives.

- § 130 § *Other parish staff members promote and support the faith formation of adults, and they encourage parish adults to participate in basic and continuous education in the faith.* All staff members promote ongoing adult faith formation and help to shape and support the policies and priorities that guide it. They work with the pastoral council and other parish leaders to make this ministry integral to parish identity and mission and a source of support for all the other ministries.

- § 131 § *The parish places adult catechesis at the center of its stated mission and goals, and it promotes the importance of adult faith formation at every opportunity.* The vision of faith formation as a lifelong journey coupled with opportunities to promote that journey hold a prominent place in strategic planning efforts, in the formulation of mission statements, and in the determination of annual goals. In addition, the parish pastoral council and other leadership bodies accept, support, promote, and participate in this vision in their work of leading and serving the parish.

- § 132 § *The parish gives adult faith formation a priority in the allocation of financial resources, in providing learning space, and in parish scheduling.* Because of its pivotal importance, parishes make a serious investment in the faith formation of adults. This includes providing facilities well adapted for adults—warm, hospitable surroundings where adults can comfortably gather, socialize, and learn together in small and large groups—whether at the parish or in the larger community (i.e., local community center). Adult faith formation is given due priority when parish facilities are scheduled and the parish calendar is drawn up. It also means providing funds for equipment—VCRs, TVs, computers—whose use will enhance adult growth.

- § 133 § *The parish helps to provide access to various available learning resources and opportunities for adults.* Parishes make available adult catechetical resources whose content is in conformity with the Scriptures and the *Catechism*, and whose approaches are consistent with the *General Directory for Catechesis.* These include print, audio, and video resources, along with training in the use of modern educational resources using computer technology.[98] A parish library is a great asset for this purpose.

§ 134 § Parishes connect parishioners to the resources of the wider community, especially diocesan conferences for catechists and pastoral leaders, programs presented in neighboring parishes or elsewhere in the diocese, and formation opportunities provided by "the various groups, movements and associations which offer catechesis for adults."[99] Appropriate programs provided by Catholic or secular colleges, night schools, adult or continuing education programs, and distance learning programs are made known to parishioners.

The Adult Faith Formation Leader

§ 135 § *Objective Two:*
> *Each parish will designate an adult faith formation leader—*
> *authorized by the pastor and personally involved in ongoing formation—to assume*
> *primary responsibility for implementing the ministry of adult faith formation.*

Each parish needs a lead agent to take hands-on responsibility "for effectively establishing the overall adult learning context and programming in the diocese/parish."[100] This person may be a member of the parish staff or a parishioner prepared for leadership in this ministry. While the position may be full-time salaried, it could just as well be filled by a person who donates his or her time for a few hours a week. What is important is that the person have or acquire an adult catechetical vision and competency, be formed by the word of God, and be well versed in and comfortable with current catechetical documents, especially the *Catechism* and the *General Directory for Catechesis.* This leader will possess the time, energy, and commitment to drive the adult learning agenda of the parish.

§ 136 § If the designated leader is the parish director of religious education or another staff person, adjustments may be needed in job descriptions so as not to shortchange the amount and quality of time and energy they can devote to adult faith formation. Otherwise their many responsibilities may prevent them from devoting sufficient time to this essential priority. We acknowledge gratefully the valuable work over the years of so many parish staff members, especially directors of religious education, who have often taken the lead in providing for adult catechesis in their places of ministry.

§ 137 § If the adult faith formation leader is not a staff member, he or she reports to the parish staff member most directly responsible for catechesis, so as to assure a cohesive parish catechetical ministry.

INDICATORS

- § 138 § *The parish designates a staff person or qualified lay parishioner as the adult faith formation leader.* The designated leader helps to shape and implement the parish's vision for lifelong growth in faith. The parish makes every effort to provide the leader suitable formation in theology, pastoral and educational skills, and spiritual development.

- § 139 § *The leader advocates for the primacy of adult faith formation in the parish.* With the guidance and support of the pastor and the parish staff, the leader directs and coordinates a comprehensive approach to parish adult faith formation.

- § 140 § *The leader promotes the development of an effective adult faith formation team.* In consultation with pastor and staff, the leader recruits and prepares an adult faith formation team. The leader helps the team find, select, and use quality resources for their own formation and for parish programs. The leader acts as a bridge connecting the team, the parish staff, other parish and diocesan groups, agencies, and service organizations.

- § 141 § *The leader works with other parish ministers to promote cohesive, effective adult faith formation programming.* The leader helps every parish ministry, program, and activity realize its full adult faith formation potential. The leader does this in a way that promotes cooperation and not competition among parish ministries.

The Adult Faith Formation Team

§ 142 § *Objective Three:*
The parish will have a core team of parishioners committed to and responsible for implementing the parish vision and plan for adult faith formation.

Providing effective, diverse adult faith formation opportunities is a demanding responsibility requiring the collaborative efforts of a well-trained, coordinated team of parishioners, "a nucleus of mature Christians, initiated into the faith."[101] Clearly, no person acting alone can adequately meet the needs and fulfill the potential of parish adult faith formation ministry. The value of a team approach has been clearly shown in the success of the RCIA, youth ministry, and pro-life activities in parishes throughout the country.

§ 143 § Working with the adult faith formation leader, the team is responsible for "coordinating the establishment of a context for adult learning, and planning activities for specific programs."[102] Its role is consultation, planning, and program implementation for adult faith formation in the parish. Typically comprising three to ten members, teams include qualified representatives of all the major parish demographic and cultural groups. This representative team will recognize the gifts and talents of each group and address the varied learning needs and interests of the multi-cultural and generational community more effectively. The adult faith formation team is encouraged to coordinate its efforts with those of other parish ministries engaged in formation (e.g., children and youth catechesis, young adult ministry, family life, pro-life, liturgy, social action, and ecumenism) in order to weave diverse parish efforts into a more cohesive approach.

- § **144** § *The parish has a functioning adult faith formation team that is formally recognized in the parish leadership structure.* The team, authorized by the pastor, has clear operating procedures and lines of accountability. Until a well-prepared team is in place, the adult faith formation leader arranges for programs and services.

- § **145** § *The parish team, working with the pastor and parish staff, formulates a vision of adult faith formation for the parish.* The team works collaboratively to identify the principal spiritual and human needs of adult parishioners, discern the learning possibilities inherent in those needs, and develop a vision and plan for parish adult faith formation. In this process the team works with the pastor and staff, draws upon its knowledge of the parish and its history and culture, and studies relevant church documents and available research on the parish and on adult catechesis.

- § **146** § *The team identifies elements of parish life that foster adult growth in faith, assesses their impact, and, if necessary, offers recommendations to enhance their effectiveness.* The parish touches the lives of adults in countless ways that shape their faith. The team becomes conscious and intentional about these aspects of parish life, evaluates their effectiveness, and offers to the staff or to the other ministry teams suggestions and assistance to make them more effective.

- § **147** § *The team provides a diverse range of quality programming for parish adult faith formation.* The team plans, promotes, implements, and evaluates suitable adult learning programs and opportunities for spiritual growth, human development, and Christian service for all members of the community.

- § **148** § *The team receives both initial and ongoing formation to prepare it to accomplish its mission effectively.* Providing quality adult catechesis requires specialized knowledge and skills. The adult faith formation leader sees that the team receives both initial orientation and ongoing formation, so that they grow in personal spirituality, love for Christ, and knowledge of the principles and methods of effective adult catechesis.

The Catechist of Adults

§ **149** § *Objective Four:*
> *Each parish will have access to trained catechists to serve the diverse adult faith formation efforts of the parish or region.*

The catechist of adults, the person "who actually engages the learners . . . is responsible for either directly presenting some facet of the Christian faith, or [for] serving as a catalyst or guide to the learners as they seek to deepen their faith."[103] All aspects of the formation of catechists must be thoroughly centered on Jesus Christ, be permeated by the Church's understanding of the Gospel, and help them learn to communicate the Good News faithfully and effectively.[104]

§ **150** § Catechists of adults need to be people of faith with an evangelizing spirit, a zeal for God's kingdom, and a commitment to lifelong formation. They have a sound grasp of

Catholic doctrine and theology, an ability to access the various sources of the word of God,[105] and an understanding of how to communicate this knowledge effectively to adults, drawing appropriately upon psychology and the social sciences as needed. They are first people of prayer who recognize their own need to grow in faith.

§ 151 § It is not enough for catechists to know their subjects. They also need the competence to animate a shared journey with other adults, the ability to relate authentic Catholic faith to real-life circumstances, the ability to guide them in prayer and through spiritual experiences, and the craft to integrate divergent tendencies into the full faith and life of the Church. It is essential that catechists witness in their own lives the truth of the faith they are communicating. This will require a love for people, a passion for catechesis, effective interpersonal and community-building skills, respect for different adult learning styles, the ability to communicate and explore the Gospel with others using active and engaging methods appropriate to the learners and to the content, and the flexibility to adapt to ever-changing circumstances.

INDICATORS

- § 152 § *Each parish has access to various types of well-prepared catechists for adult faith formation.*[106] Qualified catechists are available to work with adults in all parishes. Diocesan offices provide assistance in the formation of adult catechists and in helping parishes share qualified catechists of adults. Adult catechists are enrolled in or have completed the formation programs and requirements as determined by the local Church.

- § 153 § *Parishes provide recognition for their catechists of adults and funding assistance for their formation.* "Always and in every way, lay catechists should be *recognized, respected and loved* by their priests and communities. They should be supported in their formation and encouraged and helped to accomplish a task which is indispensable but far from easy."[107]

DIOCESAN SUPPORT FOR ADULT FAITH FORMATION

§ 154 § While the parish is the place of front-line ministry in adult faith formation, the bishop has primary responsibility for the general welfare of the local Church, and as teacher of the faith, he is the chief catechist of adults.[108] To assist the bishop in carrying out this role, the task of supporting parish adult faith formation ministers is exercised normally by diocesan administrative offices, chiefly the diocesan catechetical office.[109]

The Diocesan Vision of Adult Faith Formation

§ 155 § *Objective Five:*
> *The diocese will have a clearly stated vision of lifelong learning in parishes that promotes adult faith formation as the chief form of catechesis.*[110]

When adult faith formation is clearly at the heart of the bishop's diocesan vision for catechesis, this guides and orients all ministry agencies within the diocese toward faithful implementation of the Church's contemporary understanding of catechetical ministry.

INDICATORS

- § 156 § *The bishop is known as a consistent advocate for the centrality of adult faith formation and as a teacher of adults.* By clearly affirming and consistently promoting adult formation, the bishop sets the tone throughout the diocese. He does this by "putting into operation the necessary personnel, means, and equipment, and also the financial resources" to promote and sustain in his diocese a real passion for adult catechesis. He is "vigilant with regard to the authenticity of the faith,"[111] formation for catechists of adults, and the quality of adult catechetical materials. He is also zealous in his responsibility to "transmit personally to [the] faithful the doctrine of life"[112] in his role as preacher and teacher.

- § 157 § *The diocese gives clear priority to the formation of mature disciples of Jesus.* The diocese highlights adult faith formation and affirms its centrality in the ministry of the word.

- § 158 § *The diocese has in place a pastoral plan for adult faith formation that has been formed in consultation with diocesan and parish leaders.* A specific diocesan plan for adult faith formation, created in consultation with pastors and other parish leaders throughout the diocese, guides diocesan activities.

- § 159 § *Diocesan offices work collaboratively to advocate for a comprehensive integrated ministry of adult faith formation at the parish and inter-parish level.* All diocesan offices and agencies are concerned in their own way with fostering mature adult faith. By coordinating their plans and objectives and collaborating together, offices avoid duplicating services and unhealthy competition.

The Diocesan Plan and Strategy for Adult Faith Formation

§ 160 § *Objective Six:*
The diocese will have a clear strategy for developing parish
adult faith formation leaders, teams, and catechists.

The primary role of the diocese is to affirm the priority of adult faith formation and to provide leadership, personnel, services, and resources to assist parishes in developing this ministry. While the specifics of strategies will vary from diocese to diocese, it is crucial that parishes have reliable assistance from their diocesan offices in forming parish leadership, teams, and catechists for adult faith formation.

INDICATORS

- § 161 § *The diocese builds community and connections among parish adult faith formation leaders, and it provides for their ongoing formation and support.* Diocesan leaders take great care to nourish the faith and the skills of parish adult faith formation leaders. A network of such leaders is established across the diocese for their mutual support and enrichment.

- § 162 § *The diocese supports parish adult faith formation teams in various ways.* The diocese regularly promotes the growth of parish adult faith formation teams, advocates for them, consults with them, and offers ongoing resourcing and training.

- § 163 § *The diocese offers formation opportunities for catechists of adults.* "The formation of catechists is responsibly directed by the local Church, under the guidance of the bishop and the appropriate offices, commissions and institutes of formation, in accordance with approved principles and programs."[113]

Diocesan Support for Adult Faith Formation

§ 164 § *Objective Seven:*
> *The diocese will allocate adequate personnel and resources for carrying out the mission of adult faith formation in the diocese.*

If dioceses expect parishes to invest in adult faith formation as a priority, then dioceses must do the same.

INDICATORS

- § 165 § *The diocese has a staff person whose primary responsibility is to provide for the training and resourcing of parish adult faith formation leaders, teams, and catechists.*[114] Depending on the size and needs of the diocese, all or a significant portion of at least one designated staff person's responsibilities includes advocacy, consultation, networking, communicating, resourcing, research, and training for effective adult faith formation ministry in the diocese. Working with a diocesan commission, advisory committee, or resource network, this person directs and coordinates the various diocesan adult faith formation initiatives.

- § 166 § *The diocese has an adult faith formation commission, advisory committee, or resource network.* Members of this commission serve as a diocesan advisory body in the ministry of adult faith formation. As such, they support and assist the diocesan staff person and the parishes in various projects: the assessment of current needs; the development of a diocesan adult faith formation plan; formation for leaders, teams, and catechists; consultation with parish catechetical leaders; networking or mentoring arrangements; and reviewing and recommending materials. This commission serves as a sounding board and think tank on issues and trends. Membership is drawn from clergy, religious, and laity and from parish leadership, diocesan staff, and others with expertise in this ministry. This commission is representative of the cultural and linguistic diversity of the diocese, and it is informed about relevant church documents that address faith formation within specific cultural and ethnic Catholic communities.

- § 167 § *The diocese maintains current faith formation resources and makes them available for parish review and use.* Parishes have direct access to adult faith formation resources through publishers, bookstores, libraries, conferences, and the Internet. The diocese maintains a resource center where materials can be previewed, purchased, or borrowed.[115] The resource center also helps adult faith formation leaders and catechists learn to use media effectively with adults. All parishes—no matter what their financial situation—have access to quality materials and effective programs.

A Call to Implementation

§ 168 § The implementation of this pastoral plan can bring about profound transformation and renewal in our nation, our dioceses, and our parishes. But the plan needs to be embraced first by diocesan and parish leaders, embodied in pastoral structures and services, and put into practice by well-prepared ministers. Here are steps to take to begin this process of implementation.

§ 169 § 1) **Study the plan**, pray about it, and discuss it with others. Take time to explore its vision and initiatives. Discover how you can support the plan and how the plan can support you and others in your various ministries. Commit yourself to its implementation.

§ 170 § 2) **Analyze the situation** in which adults actually live in Church and society. Carefully research and assess the current state of affairs in adult faith formation and pastoral life in both parish and diocese. Consider how socio-cultural and economic factors, local needs and resources, the formulation of options, and existing priorities influence the implementation of this plan.[116]

§ 171 § 3) **Develop action steps** for implementing the plan. As dioceses and parishes determine their prioritized goals, objectives, and strategies for adult faith formation—flowing from the mission of the Church and the analysis of the local situation—an effective plan of action will emerge. The implementation of this plan will be characterized by its realism, simplicity, conciseness, and clarity. Such a plan will set a course for action that will generate enthusiasm within the local Church.[117]

§ 172 § The plan will address the needs of the whole community, for "the true subject of catechesis is the Church."[118] It will do this especially by attending to the various relational networks and populations in the parish. Ultimately, it will reach to the heart and mind of the individual adult and his or her need for primary proclamation, basic catechesis, or continuing education in the faith. When individuals and small communities seek out the formation they need—and when parishes have oriented their ministries to provide it—then adult faith formation will be a true priority.

§ 173 § 4) **Prepare your leaders.** Identify, invite, train, and support people to serve as lead agents in fulfilling the plan. All who serve in this ministry, whether full-time professionals, active parishioners, or outside speakers and consultants, need adequate formation.

§ 174 § Dioceses are encouraged to develop certification programs for adult faith formation ministry that offer well-planned, comprehensive, and practical training to meet the diverse needs of adults. It is essential that adult faith formation principles be incorporated into the training of future clergy, religious, and lay ministers and into all continuing formation for clergy and religious. Theology and religious studies programs that prepare persons for ministry are challenged to develop in their students competencies for working with adults and an understanding of the adult life cycle.

§ 175 § We ask that all ministry preparation and formation programs—whether under parish, inter-parish, or diocesan auspices, in seminaries, novitiates, or Catholic colleges and universities—address the importance of adult faith formation ministry and conduct their programs in accord with its principles.

§ 176 § We give thanks for all of the resources we have at our disposal. The Catholic publishing community is strong and willing to develop quality catechetical materials for adults. Their contribution to the vitality of catechetical ministry in our country with children deserves our recognition. We need and welcome their ongoing contribution to this revitalization of faith formation ministry with adults.

§ 177 § Catholic institutions of higher education and Catholic campus ministry at secular institutions are a great blessing. They have always served the Church well by educating and forming young adult Catholics. We turn to them now to help us develop creative ways of implementing this plan at parish and diocesan levels.

§ 178 § 5) **Make a commitment of financial resources.** It is not enough to talk about the need for adult faith formation; actions are also essential. Budgets and personnel decisions will need to be reconsidered in light of this plan. The challenge will be to provide resources to build adult faith without undermining other educational activities already engaged.

A Time to Plan, a Time to Act

§ 179 § We recognize that this plan cannot be implemented all at once. Time must be taken to understand the plan, carefully analyze local situations, and prepare diocesan and parish action steps. It will take at least one year before local plans can be put into effect.

§ 180 § Once the plan has been implemented in dioceses and parishes across the country, it will take several years before our labors begin to bear fruit. Five years after this plan is implemented, let us analyze our progress in making adult faith formation a true priority, assess the impact of this reorientation on the vitality of parish life and mission, and celebrate the good that has been accomplished, revising plans as needed. Every five years thereafter, let us continue to assess the situation, update plans, and renew our commitment to ongoing adult faith formation.

Conclusion

So they set out at once and returned to Jerusalem
where they found gathered together
the eleven and those with them. . . .
Then the two recounted what had taken place
on the way and how he was made known to them
in the breaking of the bread. (LK 24:33-35)

OUR HOPE FOR THE FUTURE

§ 181 § Before meeting the risen Lord on the road to Emmaus, the disciples were discouraged by all that had happened. We too, at times, may feel discouraged when our efforts do not achieve the fruitfulness for which we hope and pray. There are many obstacles to adult catechesis, many challenges to overcome to bring the living word of God to the adults in our faith communities. But just like the disciples after Jesus revealed himself to them, our hearts burn within us to proclaim the Good News of the reign of God. We are committed to this plan and are willing "to exercise utmost *courage and patience*"[119] as we implement it.

§ 182 § We move ahead full of hope, knowing this vision of adult faith formation can become reality. Jesus the Risen One is still with us, meeting us on the pathways of our lives, sharing our concerns, enlightening us with his word, strengthening us with his presence, nourishing us in the breaking of the bread, and sending us forth to be his witnesses. In the providence of God the Father, the action of the Holy Spirit will rekindle the fire of love in the hearts of the faithful and renew the catechetical dynamism of the Church.[120]

§ 183 § Awakened and energized by the Spirit, let us strengthen our commitment and intensify our efforts to help the adults in our communities be touched and transformed by the life-giving message of Jesus, to explore its meaning, experience its power, and live in its light as faithful adult disciples today. Let us do our part with creativity and vigor, our hearts aflame with love to empower adults to know and live the message of Jesus. This is the Lord's work. In the power of the Spirit it will not fail but will bear lasting fruit for the life of the world.

Afterword

§ 184 § **R**eaders of church documents and the professional literature will find different terms used to name the ministry: for example, adult catechesis, adult religious education, adult Christian education, and adult faith formation. Sometimes these terms are used more or less interchangeably, sometimes in distinction to one another.

§ 185 § We recognize that the term "catechesis" has a long history in Christian usage, and "has undergone a semantic evolution during the twenty centuries of the Church's history."[121] In most recent church documents, catechesis is understood as a moment in the process of evangelization.[122] *Adult Catechesis in the Christian Community* (1990) summarizes the usage of John Paul II in *Catechesi Tradendae* (1979) by stating, "The specific role of the catechesis of adults consists in an initial deepening of the faith received at baptism, in an elementary, complete and systematic way (CT, no. 21), with a view to helping individuals all life long grow to the full maturity of Christ (cf. Eph 4:13)."[123]

§ 186 § The text continues: "Catechesis *per se* has to be *distinguished* therefore from other activities, even though it cannot be separated from them:—it is different from evangelization, which is the proclamation of the Gospel for the first time to those who have not heard it, or the re-evangelization of those who have forgotten it;—it is different from formal religious education, which goes beyond the basic elements of faith in more systematic and specialized courses;—it is also different from those informal occasions for faith awareness in God's presence, which arise in fragmentary and incidental ways in the daily life of adults."[124]

§ 187 § More recently, the *General Directory for Catechesis* (1997) speaks of "the primary proclamation" that is addressed to nonbelievers, marginal Christians, non-Christians, and the children of Christian families; "initiatory catechesis" (also called "basic catechesis") for catechumens, candidates completing their initiation, returning Catholics, Catholic children and youth, as well as Christian education in families and religious instruction in schools; and "continuous education in the faith" ("permanent catechesis" or "continuing catechesis") for all Christians "who need constantly to nourish and deepen their faith throughout their lives." These latter two may also be called "pre- and post-baptismal catechesis." There is also a liturgical form and a theological form of the ministry of the word, and the "religious instruction" that takes place in schools.[125]

§ 188 § These various distinctions and usages are not consistently observed in all church documents, nor are they consistently used in pastoral planning and practice in our country. A clear consensus on precise contemporary terminology and usage has not yet developed, and at this time we do not wish to foreclose this natural and gradual process of development.

§ 189 § Consequently, in the present document we do not attempt to use the various distinctions with strict consistency. Rather, we have generally used the phrase "adult faith formation" to designate the whole field without further specific distinctions (i.e., catechesis, religious education, initiatory or basic catechesis, permanent catechesis or continuous education in the faith, and perfective catechesis).

§ **190** § At the same time we also acknowledge the usefulness of knowing these various distinctions. They can assist planners to be aware of the many different faith needs and circumstances of adults in their community and to offer them a wide and relevant range of programming and services suited to their particular faith itinerary.

§ **191** § We encourage further reflection on this issue, with the aim of helping practitioners better name their multiform ministry and better identify and serve the unique circumstances and diverse needs of the individuals and groups on whose behalf they are charged to minister God's word.

Notes

1 Cf. Congregation for the Clergy, *General Directory for Catechesis* (GDC), nos. 121, 124 (Washington, D.C.: United States Catholic Conference, 1998).

2 Cf. GDC, no. 136.

3 On the term "adult faith formation," please see the Afterword (pages 85-86).

4 International Council for Catechesis, *Adult Catechesis in the Christian Community: Some Principles and Guidelines* (ACCC), no 25 (Washington, D.C.: United States Catholic Conference, 1992).

5 GDC, no. 275; cf. Congregation for the Clergy, *General Catechetical Directory* (GCD), no. 20 (Washington, D.C.: United States Catholic Conference, 1971).

6 GDC, no. 50; cf. Paul VI, *Evangelii Nuntiandi: On Evangelization in the Modern World* (EN), nos. 42-45, 54, 57 (Washington, D.C.: United States Catholic Conference, 1975).

7 GDC, no. 59, citing GCD, no. 20; John Paul II, *Catechesi Tradendae: On Catechesis in Our Time* (CT), no. 43 (Washington, D.C.: United States Catholic Conference, 1979), cf. Part 4, Chapter 2.

8 Cf. GDC, nos. 224-225; *Code of Canon Law* (CIC), nos. 773, 776-777 (Washington, D.C.: Canon Law Society of America, 1983); *Code of Canons of the Eastern Churches* (CCEO) (1990), nos. 617, 619, 624; CT, no. 64; United States Catholic Conference, *Sharing the Light of Faith: National Catechetical Directory for Catholics of the United States* (NCD), no. 217 (Washington, D.C.: United States Catholic Conference, 1979); Second Vatican Council, *Presbyterorum Ordinis: Decree on the Ministry and Life of Priests* (PO), no. 6. In *Vatican Council II: The Conciliar and Post Conciliar Documents: New Revised Edition*, ed. Austin Flannery (Northport, N.Y.: Costello Publishing Co., 1992).

9 Second Vatican Council, *Lumen Gentium: Dogmatic Constitution on the Church* (LG), no. 25. In *Vatican Council II: The Conciliar and Post Conciliar Documents: New Revised Edition*, ed. Austin Flannery (Northport, N.Y.: Costello Publishing Co., 1992); CT, no. 63; GDC, nos. 222-223.

10 Cf. ACCC, no. 82; GDC, nos. 265-267.

11 John Paul II, *Redemptoris Missio: On the Permanent Validity of the Church's Missionary Mandate* (RM), no. 3 (Washington, D.C.: United States Catholic Conference, 1991).

12 Cf. Second Vatican Council, *Apostolicam Actuositatem: Decree on the Apostolate of Lay People* (AA), no. 4. In *Vatican Council II: The Conciliar and Post Conciliar Documents: New Revised Edition*, ed. Austin Flannery (Northport, N.Y.: Costello Publishing Co., 1992).

13 CT, no. 43.

14 Ibid.

15 GDC, nos. 59, 171, 275.

16 United States Catholic Conference, Department of Education, *Serving Life and Faith: Adult Religious Education and the American Catholic Community*, no. 157 (Washington, D.C.: United States Catholic Conference, 1986).

[17] U.S. Catholic Bishops, *To Teach as Jesus Did: A Pastoral Message on Catholic Education*, no. 43 (Washington, D.C.: United States Catholic Conference, 1972).

[18] NCD, no. 40.

[19] Cf. Jn 10:10; *Catechism of the Catholic Church* (CCC), no. 1996ff. (Washington, D.C.: United States Catholic Conference, 2000).

[20] Cf. CCC, nos. 1023ff., 1042ff.

[21] Cf. CCC, no. 150.

[22] U.S. Catholic Bishops, *Called and Gifted for the Third Millennium: Reflections of the U.S. Catholic Bishops on the Thirtieth Anniversary of the "Decree on the Apostolate of the Laity" and the Fifteenth Anniversary of "Called and Gifted"* (CGTM) (Washington, D.C.: United States Catholic Conference, 1995), p. 20; cf. GDC, nos. 53-57.

[23] GDC, no. 173.

[24] GDC, no. 82; cf. GDC, nos. 56c, 66; CIC, no. 773; CCEO, no. 617; Second Vatican Council, *Christus Dominus: Decree on the Pastoral Office of Bishops in the Church*, no. 14. In *Vatican Council II: The Conciliar and Post Conciliar Documents: New Revised Edition*, ed. Austin Flannery (Northport, N.Y.: Costello Publishing Co., 1992).

[25] Cf. CCC, nos. 153-154.

[26] AA, no. 4; cf. GDC, nos. 51, 85; CCC, nos. 1074, 1123.

[27] CCC, no. 158, citing St. Anselm, *Prosl. prooem.* In *Patrologia Latina*, nos. 153, 225a, ed. J. P. Migne (Paris: 1841-1855).

[28] Cf. GDC, no. 56a-b.

[29] LG, no. 8.

[30] CCC, no. 163.

[31] CCC, no. 2820; cf. CCC, nos. 1049, 2818; Second Vatican Council, *Gaudium et Spes: Pastoral Constitution on the Church in the Modern World* (GS), nos. 21, 34, 39, 43, 57, 72. In *Vatican Council II: The Conciliar and Post Conciliar Documents: New Revised Edition*, ed. Austin Flannery (Northport, N.Y.: Costello Publishing Co., 1992).

[32] GDC, no. 53; cf. CT, no. 5b; cf. CCC, nos. 422-429.

[33] Cf. Second Vatican Council, *Dei Verbum: Dogmatic Constitution on Divine Revelation* (DV), no. 8. In *Vatican Council II: The Conciliar and Post Conciliar Documents: New Revised Edition*, ed. Austin Flannery (Northport, N.Y.: Costello Publishing Co., 1992); CCC, no. 94.

[34] GDC, no. 82.

[35] GDC, no. 99.

[36] CCC, no. 259; cf. CT, no. 5.

[37] John Paul II, *Christifideles Laici: The Vocation and the Mission of the Lay Faithful in the Church and in the World*, no. 64 (Washington, D.C.: United States Catholic Conference, 1988).

[38] CCC, no. 157; cf. 1 Thes 2:13.

39 LG, no. 12.

40 CT, no. 61.

41 GS, no. 92; cf. John Paul II, "Eighth Address of His Holiness Pope John Paul II to the Bishops of the United States during Their *Ad Limina* Visits," *Ad Limina Addresses: The Addresses of His Holiness Pope John Paul II to the Bishops of the United States during Their* Ad Limina *Visits: March 5–December 9, 1988* (Washington, D.C.: United States Catholic Conference, 1988); John XXIII, *Ad Petri Cathedram* (*On Truth, Unity and Peace*), 1959.

42 Cf. Second Vatican Council, *Gravissimum Educationis: Declaration on Christian Education*, no. 2. In *Vatican Council II: The Conciliar and Post Conciliar Documents: New Revised Edition*, ed. Austin Flannery (Northport, N.Y.: Costello Publishing Co., 1992); CIC, no. 217; CCEO, no. 20.

43 ACCC, no. 35.

44 CCC, no. 426, citing CT, no. 5; cf. GDC, nos. 36-43.

45 ACCC, no. 36.

46 EN, no. 23.

47 ACCC, no. 37.

48 ACCC, no. 38.

49 ACCC, no. 24.

50 Cf. GS, no. 39.

51 John Paul II, *Familiaris Consortio: On the Family*, Part 3 (Washington, D.C.: United States Catholic Conference, 1982); U.S. Catholic Bishops' Ad Hoc Committee on Marriage and Family Life, *A Family Perspective in Church and Society: A Manual for All Pastoral Leaders*, Chapter 4 (Washington, D.C.: United States Catholic Conference, 1988); cf. GDC, nos. 226-227, 255.

52 ACCC, no. 29.

53 Cf. GDC, nos. 59, 275.

54 Pontifical Council for Social Communications, *Aetatis Novae: A New Era: Pastoral Instruction on Social Communication* (AN), no. 8 (Washington, D.C.: United States Catholic Conference, 1992).

55 Cf. GDC, nos. 189-190.

56 Cf. GDC, nos. 59, 68, 88-91.

57 ACCC, no. 66; cf. GDC, no. 68.

58 ACCC, no. 56.

59 ACCC, no. 28.

60 CT, no. 53; GDC, nos. 109, 202.

61 The use of the word "culture" here is broader than ethnicity. There are many types of cultures present in the United States including those of various regions, economic classes, religions, and age groupings.

62 Cf. CT, no. 53.

[63] RM, no. 54; GDC, no. 206, cf. no. 109.

[64] GDC, no. 127, citing DV, no. 21.

[65] GDC, no. 120.

[66] Cf. GDC, no. 136.

[67] GDC, no. 87, cf. nos. 84-86.

[68] ACCC, no. 43.

[69] CCC, no. 2597.

[70] CCC, no. 1970; cf. Jn 15:12, 13:34.

[71] GDC, no. 85.

[72] GDC, no. 35; cf. Bishops' Committee on the Liturgy, *Rite of Christian Initiation of Adults: Study Edition* (RCIA), no. 78 (Washington, D.C.: United States Catholic Conference, 1988).

[73] GDC, no. 262a.

[74] GDC, no. 54; CCC, no. 177; NCD, no. 56; GCD, no. 36.

[75] CIC, no. 773; CCEO, no. 617; GDC, no. 87.

[76] GDC, no. 51, citing GCD, no. 19d.

[77] CCC, no. 1343.

[78] Second Vatican Council, *Sacrosanctum Concilium: The Constitution on the Sacred Liturgy*, no. 14. In *Vatican Council II: The Conciliar and Post Conciliar Documents: New Revised Edition*, ed. Austin Flannery (Northport, N.Y.: Costello Publishing Co., 1992).

[79] GDC, no. 207.

[80] GDC, no. 226, citing CT, no. 68; cf. GDC, nos. 226-227; NCD, no. 221a.

[81] Pontifical Council for Social Communications, *Communio et Progressio: Pastoral Instruction on the Means of Social Communication*, no. 48 (Washington, D.C.: United States Catholic Conference, 1971).

[82] CGTM, p. 11.

[83] GDC, no. 263; RM, no. 51; cf. GDC, nos. 258c, 264.

[84] GDC, no. 275, cf. no. 56d.

[85] GDC, no. 234.

[86] GDC, no. 158.

[87] GDC, no. 257, cf. no. 158.

[88] NCD, no. 189.

[89] Cf. GDC, nos. 51, 57.

90 CT, no. 48; cf. GDC, no. 70.

91 Peter L. Benson and Carolyn H. Eklin, *Effective Christian Education: A National Study of Protestant Congregations* (Minneapolis, Minn.: Search Institute, 1990).

92 James Davidson et al., *The Search for Common Ground* (Huntington, Ind.: Our Sunday Visitor, 1997).

93 CIC, nos. 519, 528.1, 776-777; CCEO, nos. 282, 289, 619, 624; cf. GDC, nos. 224-225, 232.

94 GDC, no. 234; cf. ACCC, no. 83.

95 GDC, no. 225.

96 GDC, no. 224, citing PO, no. 6b.

97 GDC, no. 56d.

98 AN, nos. 11, 18; cf. ACCC, no. 65.

99 ACCC, no. 84.

100 *Ministering to Adult Learners: A Skills Workbook for Christian Educational Leaders*, ed. Jane Wolford Hughes (Washington, D.C.: United States Catholic Conference, 1981), p. 29.

101 GDC, no. 258c.

102 *Ministering to Adult Learners*, p. 23.

103 Ibid., p. 17.

104 GDC, nos. 235-236.

105 Cf. GDC, nos. 95-96; CCC, no. 11; ACCC, no. 39; NCD, no. 41; GCD, no. 45; CIC, no. 760; CCEO, no. 615.

106 Cf. GDC, nos. 176, 232; ACCC, nos. 74, 77.

107 ACCC, no. 76; cf. Congregation for the Evangelization of Peoples, *Guide for Catechists* (GC), no. 27 (Washington, D.C.: United States Catholic Conference, 1993).

108 ACCC, no. 82; cf. CT, no. 63.

109 Cf. GDC, nos. 265-267; NCD, nos. 218b, 238c; *Those Who Hear You Hear Me: A Resource for Bishops and Diocesan Educational/Catechetical Leaders* (Washington, D.C.: United States Catholic Conference, 1995).

110 Cf. GDC, no. 59.

111 GDC, no. 223.

112 CT, no. 63.

113 ACCC, no. 80; cf. GDC, no. 234; NCD, no. 218b5-6.

114 Cf. ACCC, no. 82.

115 Cf. GC, no. 30.

116 GDC, no. 279; cf. GDC, nos. 266a, 279-280; GCD, nos. 98.1, 99-102.

117 GDC, no. 281; cf. GDC, nos. 266b, 103-107.

118 GDC, no. 78; cf. GDC, nos. 51, 57, 60ff.

119 ACCC, no. 85.

120 Cf. CT, no. 72.

121 GDC, no. 35.

122 Cf. CT, no. 18; GDC, no. 63.

123 ACCC, no. 32.

124 Ibid.

125 GDC, nos. 51-76; cf. ACCC, corresponding to "evangelization."